Principia Meta-Ethica

Principia Meta-Ethica

CALVIN P. VAN REKEN

☙PICKWICK *Publications* · Eugene, Oregon

PRINCIPIA META-ETHICA

Copyright © 2015 Calvin P. Van Reken. All rights reserved. Except for brief quotations in critical publications or reviews, no part of this book may be reproduced in any manner without prior written permission from the publisher. Write: Permissions, Wipf and Stock Publishers, 199 W. 8th Ave., Suite 3, Eugene, OR 97401.

Pickwick Publications
An Imprint of Wipf and Stock Publishers
199 W. 8th Ave., Suite 3
Eugene, OR 97401

www.wipfandstock.com

ISBN 13: 978-1-4982-2476-5

Cataloguing-in-Publication data:

Van Reken, Calvin Paul, 1949–.

    Principia meta-ethica / Calvin P. Van Reken.

    xii + 152 p. ; 23 cm. Includes bibliographical references.

    ISBN 13: 978-1-4982-2476-5

    1. Ethics. 2. Knowledge, Theory of. I. Title.

BJ37 V33 2015

Manufactured in the U.S.A.   10/21/2015

To my parents
Everett and Rose Van Reken

Contents

Preface | ix

1. Moral Reality: The Moral Order | 1
2. Moral Language | 22
3. Basic Moral Propositions | 41
4. Moral Principles | 59
5. The Moral Field: Distinguishing the Moral and the Amoral | 81
6. Moral Epistemology | 105
7. Grounding the Moral Order | 124

Bibliography | 143
Index of Topics | 145
Index of Authors | 151

Preface

In 1903 G. E. Moore published *Principia Ethica*, a seminal volume in moral philosophy. Alan Donagan, who later became my PhD advisor at the University of Chicago, assigned it as a primary text for a graduate seminar in Ethics in 1973—such was the influence of Moore's book among moral philosophers that it was still assigned as a course text 70 years later. I was impressed with Moore because of the clarity and wisdom that he brought to his subject matter, and although my moral philosophy is different from his in some respects, he was one of those who stimulated my interest in metaethics—the topic on which I wrote my PhD dissertation. I hold him in high regard as an example of clear philosophical thinking and writing.

I had the advantage of learning from and reading other clear thinkers in my undergraduate years at Calvin College. The department of philosophy at that time was blessed with exceptional thinkers and teachers like Alvin Plantinga, Richard Mouw, Nicholas Wolterstorff, Ken Konyndyk, and others. When I returned to Grand Rapids to study at Calvin Theological Seminary, I became an adjunct teacher in Calvin's philosophy department and these outstanding philosophers became my colleagues. I still remember the Tuesday afternoon philosophy department colloquia at which we first held a 15-minute business meeting, and then spent about two hours discussing a paper written by someone in the group. We would go through the paper paragraph by paragraph—the standards for clarity and truth were high, but the discussion was always carried out in a spirit of collegiality and helpfulness. Whether the views presented in the paper were obvious or disputed, the discussion was always engaging and informative. We had fun even when the paper did not fare so well; I cannot think of an occasion when we did not all leave as friends. I learned how to be a better philosopher and how to be a better colleague.

Preface

On one of these occasions I offered up a paper I had written on metaethics. I don't remember the title, but I remember that my thesis was that G. E. Moore was right when he said that ethics was an independent science and that the basic moral properties, like moral goodness, were not identical with any non-moral properties—they were *sui generis*. Moore believed his view implied that no moral predicate (which expresses a moral property) is synonymous with any non-moral predicate. When a moralist made such a claim, Moore would accuse him of committing what he called "the naturalistic fallacy." I think now that Moore is right to say that moral properties are irreducible, but they have an important and complicated relationship to certain non-moral properties. (In chapter 4 I examine this relationship more closely.) The view that no moral predicate is synonymous with any non-moral predicate is an opinion about the common meaning and use of words, and as such should really not hold much philosophic interest. (I say more about this in chapter 2.) What is of interest is not the meaning of the words, but what they refer to—and two terms can refer to the same thing without being synonymous. As I recall it, the thesis of my paper was generally accepted while my arguments for the thesis were found wanting.

The primary areas of inquiry in philosophical metaethics are moral language, moral ontology, and moral epistemology. Chapter 1 takes up a most important question in moral ontology—whether an objective and universal morality exists. What I call the *classical view* affirms it; the *postmodern view* denies it. Other questions in moral ontology are taken up in chapter 3 on Basic Moral Propositions, chapter 4 on Moral Principles, chapter 5 on the Moral Field, that is, what is moral as opposed to amoral, and chapter 7 on the Grounding of Morality. Chapter 2 considers moral language and the metaethical view called *expressivism*—an approach which I argue is mistaken. In chapter 6 moral epistemology is considered and I adapt an epistemological theory developed by Alvin Plantinga in his magisterial *Warranted Christian Belief* in order to show how it is that we can know moral truths. My hope is that this volume will kindle a renewed interest in the issues it addresses and will provoke a return to classical metaethics.

I am thankful to God for the teachers, colleagues, and friends that he has put in my life, especially for Alvin Plantinga, Richard Mouw, and Alan Donagan, each of whom were wonderful teachers, clear thinkers, and fine persons. The Lord has used each of them in important ways in my life and the lives of many others. I also thank God for my colleagues at Calvin Theological Seminary for their support and friendship over more than twenty

Preface

years, especially John Bolt, John Cooper, Arie Leder, and Richard Muller. The board of the seminary was gracious in granting me several sabbaticals during which I wrote most of this book, and I'm grateful to them as well.

Finally, two people deserve special mention. My son-in-law, Sean Christy, was a thoughtful and wise partner for the content of this book and in preparing it for publication. I am doubtful I would have finished this book without him—I know it would have had many more mistakes. And I want to thank my wife Rose, who gave me enough time and space to work on this book, who read most of it and saved me from numerous stylistic gaucheries. I don't know if it takes a village to raise a child, I have learned that it takes helpful and supportive people for me to write a book. I am grateful to them all.

I

Moral Reality
The Moral Order

In 1993 Gene Outka and John P. Reeder edited the anthology *Prospects for a Common Morality* in which a variety of moral philosophers addressed the question of whether there are any prospects for a common morality. The rough idea of a "common" morality used by Outka and Reeder is a morality that is binding on all persons (universal) and could be justified to persons in a variety of cultures.[1] Their notion of a common morality includes two parts: ontological and epistemological. Ontologically, it is a universal moral standard "by which everybody ought to live, no matter what the mores of his neighbors might be."[2] Epistemologically, it is a morality that could be justified to reasonable persons in a variety of cultures. So a common morality would be one which is both universally binding and rationally justifiable.

Two Views of the Prospects for a Common Morality

Disagreement over a common morality is an important part of what distinguishes postmodern from classical metaethics. Briefly stated, postmodern ethicists take the view that there are no prospects for establishing a common morality—a sharp departure from the classical view that there are

---

1. I begin using Outka and Reeder's terminology, but will find it helpful to introduce a number of distinctions and terms that are more clear.
2. Donagan, *Theory of Morality*, 1.

prospects for it. I will consider each of these views regarding a common morality, starting with the more familiar postmodern view.

No Prospects for a Common Morality

The view that there are no prospects for a common morality became the dominant view in Western philosophy in the latter half of the twentieth century. Some attribute the beginnings of this postmodern view to Hegel and his claim that moral principles alone (such as Kant's categorical imperative) are purely formal, devoid of moral content, and so moral principles are unable to help distinguish what is morally right and wrong. In Hegel's view what was needed to fill this void was *Sittlichkeit*, the mores of an actual community. Thus Hegel helped to move the focus of moral inquiry from the general consideration of the conduct of human persons as rational beings to the more localized questions of beings-in-community.[3] The mortal blow to the prospects of a common morality was not delivered by Hegel, but rather by Nietzsche. Gertrude Himmelfarb nicely summarizes the impact of Nietzsche on moral thought:

> It was in the 1880s that Friedrich Nietzsche began to speak of "values" in its present sense—not as a verb, meaning to value or esteem something; nor as a singular noun, meaning the measure of a thing, but in the plural, connoting the moral beliefs and attitudes of a society . . . Early in the twentieth century, shortly after Nietzsche's death, the sociologist Max Weber borrowed the word "values." . . . [It] brought with it the assumptions that all moral ideas are subjective and relative, that they are mere customs and conventions, that they have a purely instrumental, utilitarian purpose, and that they are peculiar to specific individuals and societies."[4]

One prominent contemporary philosopher who follows in the wake of Nietzsche is Richard Rorty, who is indignant at any idea of a common morality. He writes, "what counts as rational or as fanatical is relative to the group to which we think it necessary to justify ourselves—to the body of shared belief that determines the reference of the word 'we.'"[5] What is

---

3. Ibid., 10. Donagan says of Hegel's view, "[I]t follows that the proper subject of philosophical ethics is not morality but *Sittlichkeit*."

4. Himmelfarb, *Demoralization of Society*, 10–11.

5. Rorty, "Priority of Democracy," 256.

considered outrageous or fanatical behavior is always relative to a community with shared beliefs; there are no trans-cultural standards by which such judgments can be justified or condemned. This view implies that were an adult to crush the skull of a two-year-old with an axe, his act is not morally right or morally wrong in itself; rather, the fitting moral description of the act depends on the community in which the act is done. Some societies have practiced child sacrifice in order to please or appease some god or other. In such societies this was approved, and so is morally right. What practices and conduct persons engage in is neither morally right nor wrong independent of the approvals of the society—such approvals are the only way to measure the morality of any conduct. Since no act is intrinsically morally right or wrong, even Hitler's final solution cannot be said to be morally wrong *simpliciter*.[6]

Richard Rorty is not primarily an ethicist, so perhaps his views regarding common morality should not to be considered typical for a postmodern ethicist. Alasdair MacIntyre, in contrast, has been one of the most influential and important ethicists in the latter twentieth century. In *A Short History of Ethics* MacIntyre takes the view that there is no hope of shaping a morality that is justifiable to persons in a variety of cultures. He sharply criticizes the attempt to "absolutize" any morality, claiming that moral concepts are neither timeless nor unhistorical.[7] Moreover, he says there are no universally convincing reasons for believing in human rights. Human rights give rise to moral obligations, since if even one person has a right to something, then all others have a moral obligation to let that person exercise that right. So there is no common morality and there are no human rights. In some subsequent publications MacIntyre modified this view and has argued that morality does arise within a community with a shared understanding of what persons are and what virtues they ought to acquire.

---

6. In "Truth and Freedom," Rorty is dismissive of the idea that there is any meaningful way even to speak of trans-cultural moral truth, or trans-cultural truth of any sort, or even any reason to speak of truth within a community. On Rorty's view there is no connection between the way the world is and our descriptions of it in our language. Sentences are not attempts to represent reality but tools used to accomplish purposes. All that the idea of truth does is to say, "Bethink yourself that you might be mistaken; remember that your beliefs may be justified by your other beliefs in the area, but that the whole kit and kaboodle might be misguided, and in particular that you might be using the wrong words for your purpose" (280). Rorty's view of the measure of human assertions is not whether the truth is spoken, but whether the words effectively accomplish your chosen purpose or the purpose of the "we" with which you choose to include yourself.

7. MacIntyre, *A Short History*, 269.

However, since communities do not share understanding of what persons are and what virtue is there are no prospects for a common morality. This view is similar to Rorty's because it also limits the possible justification of moral claims to communities with shared ideas.

Rorty and MacIntyre are representative of the moral climate of opinion among philosophers in the second half of the twentieth century. Many others could be identified, but these two clearly illustrate the postmodern opinion regarding metaethics.

Some Prospects for a Common Morality

The alternative to the postmodern view is that there are in fact some prospects for a common morality—the classical view. This understanding of metaethics has a much longer history—it goes back 2,500 years, and is advanced by ethicists that include Plato, Aristotle, Cicero, Augustine, Aquinas, J. S. Mill, Immanuel Kant, and a host of others. More recently the view has been championed by thinkers like C. S. Lewis, Alan Donagan, and Alan Gewirth. Let's consider what just a few of these had to say about a common morality.

The Roman philosopher Cicero makes clear that there is a universal moral law for all people. "There can be but one essential justice, which cements society, and one law which establishes this justice. This law is right reason, which is the true rule of all commandments and prohibitions. Whoever neglects this law, whether written or unwritten, is necessarily unjust and wicked."[8] Cicero is very clear about the importance of grounding this universal moral law in nature, not in common opinion. As such it is not a product of human beliefs, desires, or choices. "For all the questions on which our philosophers argue, there is none which it is more important thoroughly to understand than this, that man is born for justice, and that law and equity are not a mere establishment of opinion, but an institution of nature."[9] Cicero says that his view of morality was favored by all the philosophers of Plato's old academy and those who followed Aristotle.[10] Thus the classical view in the West has its origins in antiquity and was the dominant view of metaethics until the postmodern view came into vogue.

---

8. Cicero, *De Legibus*, Book 1, 45.
9. Ibid., 45.
10. Ibid., 51–52.

Moral Reality

Augustine also thinks that there is a universal morality. Like Cicero, he identifies *justice* as the key feature of a permanent reality.

> Some . . . thought that there was no such thing as absolute justice but that every people regarded its own way of life as just. For if justice, which ought to remain immutable, varies so much among different peoples, it is evident that justice does not exist. They have not understood, to cite only one instance, that "what you do not wish to have done to yourself, do not do to another" cannot be varied on account of any diversity of peoples.[11]

Augustine notes that some may think that the fact that different societies have different ways of life and varying standards of justice leads some to the view that there is no one immutable standard of morality. He counters this by giving one example of a moral precept (the silver rule[12]) that he asserts is binding on all persons, regardless of their diversity. The implication of Augustine's view is that there are some local rules and customs that people follow, but that there is also at least one immutable precept that is common to every culture. From this it follows that if it is immutable it provides a standard with which every other local rule and custom must be logically consistent; if it is common to all societies and cultures, then they all must have rules and customs that are consistent with it.

In *Mere Christianity* C. S. Lewis notes that people share a common sense of right and wrong.[13] Everyone finds it objectionable when someone cuts in a long ticket line that is moving slowly. He observes that even individuals who theoretically deny there is an objective morality often will appeal to it when they have experienced some gross injustice. Their claim is not merely that something illegal was done, but they want to make the stronger claim that something morally wrong was done. Lewis says that all persons, in any society, have similar reactions when treated unfairly. In the appendix to *The Abolition of Man* Lewis identifies many moral precepts that are common in many societies and gives a brief compilation of them,[14] supplementing Augustine's single immutable moral precept with a dozen or so which he claims are common to many societies. Virtually every society condemns traitors, believes a person should care for her parents,

---

11. Outka, "Augustinianism," 117, quoting Augustine, *On Christian Doctrine*.
12. The silver rule is "do not do to others what you do not want them to do to you." It is the negative form of the more familiar golden rule.
13. Lewis, *Mere Christianity*, 3–7.
14. Lewis, *Abolition of Man*, 95–121.

and condones general beneficence. He claims, similarly to Augustine, that the golden rule "do to others as you would have them do to you" can be found in one form or another in more than fifteen different cultures. In making this case Lewis is agreeing with Augustine and echoing Cicero, who writes: "But in nothing is the uniformity of human nature more conspicuous than in its respect for virtue. What nation is there, in which kindness, benignity, gratitude, and mindfulness of benefits are not recommended? What nation in which arrogance, malice, cruelty, and unthankfulness, are not reprobated and detested?"[15] Lewis acknowledges that the existence of common virtues in different societies does not prove there is an immutable morality. He identifies this morality as the law of human nature and calls it the "Tao." "I am not trying to prove its [the Tao's] validity by the argument from common consent. Its validity cannot be deduced. For those who do not perceive its rationality, even universal consent would not prove it."[16]

The common acceptance of some moral precepts across different societies provides, at most, relatively weak *inductive* evidence for the reality of an immutable universal morality. It is weak evidence because there are reasons which could explain why moral precepts are common in different societies. For instance, some ways of conduct are less destructive or more life affirming than others, and precepts making them forbidden or obligatory could be expected in different societies. So personal and/or social survival may be the reason, rather than a universal morality, for precepts to be approved in different societies.

So Cicero, Augustine, and Lewis endorse the idea that there is a standard that is trans-cultural and which is binding on all people simply by virtue of their humanity. This classical view of metaethics is shared by both Christians and non-Christians.

Two Concepts of Morality

What we are left with is two ontological possibilities for metaethics: the postmodern and the classical. The postmodern view is that each moral precept exists only within a community of shared beliefs. According to the postmodern view it is possible that the same moral precept is shared in different societies, but from this fact it does not follow that those precepts are immutable in any way that transcends those societies. After all,

15. Cicero, *De Legibus*, Book 1, 47.
16. Lewis, *Abolition of Man*, 95.

any community could come to have some different beliefs that may produce some different moral precepts. Moral precepts, as such, are justifiable only so long as the beliefs within the community support them. On this view even if there were the universal acceptance of a moral precept, like the golden rule, that would be no more than an interesting coincidence in cultural history. Moral precepts are nothing more than accepted standards for conduct.

In contrast to this, the classical view is that there are moral precepts that are true and immutable. In fact, even if no culture or society accepted them, they would still be true and correct. Their correctness and truth is not a product of shared beliefs in a community or the common opinion in a society. They prescribe how every human being ought to act and are grounded on human nature. While human opinion can vary from time to time and place to place, human nature is fixed and does not change. That is a very important point for Cicero, and it is why Augustine refers to justice as an immutable law.

So there are two views of morality: the postmodern view is that moral precepts are merely grounded in social beliefs and subject to change; the classical view is that moral precepts are grounded in human nature and are universal and immutable. The term "morality" can refer to either of these two different concepts. On the one hand "morality" expresses the postmodern concept when it is used to refer to the actual customs, practices, and rules that a group or society affirms and approves. In this sense we can speak of various moralities: "the morality of the Incas" or "the morality of the Japanese;" we even speak of "business morality." On the other hand, "morality" can refer to a fixed set of rules that is binding on every person and every society, whether or not they affirm or approve these rules—the classical view.

The two concepts of morality give rise to two different understandings of a common morality. A common morality understood in the postmodern sense is a set of moral precepts that could be accepted and approved by people in all societies. The classical concept of morality is that it is binding on everyone everywhere, so if there is such a morality, it is common. Alan Gewirth notes this distinction and calls the two concepts the "positive" and the "normative" concepts of a common morality. The positive concept of a common morality is "a set of rules or directives for action that are upheld as categorically obligatory by all persons in their words or beliefs or actions."[17]

17. Gewirth, "Common Morality," 30.

The key notion here is that this morality is in fact accepted (or "upheld") by all persons. (Medieval Christian theologians such as Ulpian, Isidore of Seville, and Gratian, referred to this positive sense as *ius gentium*.) Could there be a common morality in this positive sense? Could there be any moral precepts that all people hold as binding? Cicero and C. S. Lewis say that there are some moral precepts that (virtually) all societies accept. In contrast Stanley Hauerwas, a Christian ethicist, denies that there is any common morality in this positive sense, writing "[T]here is no universal morality, but . . . in fact we live in a fragmented world of many moralities."[18] The alternative to positive morality, according to Gewirth, is a normative concept of common morality. That concept is one in which "its norms—its rules or principles—must be valid or justified for and incumbent upon all persons, so that, whether or not the norms are in fact universally upheld as valid, they ought to be thus upheld."[19] (Medieval Christian theologians referred to this as *ius naturale*.) The normative concept of a common morality is the classical view, that there is a set of precepts that is binding on all persons, regardless of whether every person or society upholds or affirms it.

Are there any prospects for a common positive morality—one that is common to all societies because all agree and hold it as binding? Hauerwas may be correct that there is no single positive morality (a set of moral precepts) that is affirmed in every society. Whether there is or could be a common morality in the positive sense is a question whose answer depends on whether it is true or possible for all people to agree on some standards for human conduct. The normative issue of whether there could be a common morality does not require groups of people or societies to agree on any standards. It is a concept of morality that it is binding on everyone whether or not they affirm it. Whether there is or could be a common positive morality—one which everyone agrees with—neither confirms nor disconfirms that there is or could be a common normative morality—one which is binding on everyone. Whether there is or could be a common normative morality neither confirms nor disconfirms that there is or could be a common positive morality. Though answers to these two questions are logically unrelated, they do have some bearing on each other. If there is a common positive morality, as C. S. Lewis and Cicero say, then that is some evidence that there is a common normative morality—since a common positive morality very well may be based on a common normative reality.

18. Hauerwas, *Peaceable Kingdom*, 60–61.
19. Ibid., 31.

One obvious possibility is that people agree on some moral issues because there really is a moral standard they all recognize. And if there is a common normative morality, then the prospects improve of people agreeing and coming to a positive morality.

It should be clear that the question that distinguishes the postmodern view and the classical view is the question of the prospects for a common normative morality. The great issue in philosophical metaethics is whether there is a standard or norm for human conduct that binding on every person everywhere whether or not they affirm or accept it. The classical view says that such a moral standard exists; the postmodern view denies it.

For clarity, I will refer to the concept of common normative morality as the *moral order*. (The classical term would be to simply call the moral order "morality," but as I have already noted, this term is now frequently used to refer to positive morality, that is, a socially accepted systems of mores.) The moral order is that set of principles and precepts that are binding on every human person who ever has lived or will live—whether or not a person accepts or approves of them.

Moral Realism and Moral Antirealism

The classical view that the moral order exists is *moral realism*; the postmodern view that there is no moral order, no universal normative standard for human conduct, is *moral antirealism*. A seminal question in metaethics is whether the moral order exists, that is, whether there is a moral reality that is binding on all human persons. The moral order, if it exists, would be expressed by the set of all true moral principles and precepts.

Moral antirealist views come in a wide range that can be herded into two general versions distinguished primarily by their views of moral language. If moral antirealism is true then there is an initial problem with how to understand moral utterances. When a person asserts a moral claim she seems to be asserting a fact. When Martha says "John's lie about his mother is morally wrong" she would seem to be saying that this person's act, John's lying about his mother, has the property of being morally impermissible. It seems to parallel other factual statements, like *the water in the pot is very hot*. In the latter case the speaker is attributing the property of *being very hot* to the water in the pot. In both cases the property referred to is based on a standard, in the moral case on a standard for evaluating morality and in the water case one for measuring water temperature. But according to moral antirealists the moral utterance and the factual utterance are not parallel. Their analysis is that to say "John's lie about his mother is morally wrong" may mean a number of different things. One view is that it is no more than saying that you personally disapprove of what he said, or perhaps that what he said makes you feel bad, or even that what John did violates the agreed upon standards for conduct in his (or your) culture. The implicit standard on which the moral utterance is based is one that is relative to each speaker or to each speaker's culture and has no universal meaning. There is no trans-cultural normative standard for the properties that such statements refer to.

To differentiate between these possibilities, moral antirealism has two main varieties—*moral constructivism* and *moral expressivism*. The difference between these two views has to do with how they explain moral language. When a moral property is attributed to an act or to a person, like *John's lie about his mother is morally impermissible*, what does it mean? Constructivism holds that moral statements are factual but refer merely to social morality. Thus when a person says "polygamy is immoral" what needs to be taken into account is the social context the speaker has in view, and the truth of it depends on the approval of polygamy in that context. It needs to be understood as the statement that "polygamy is immoral in society A" where "A" is a variable for the relevant society. The claim itself may or may not be a fact, depending on the actual mores of society A. On the constructivist view, moral reality is something that persons construct from what they believe is binding regarding conduct; so constructivists think moral statements refer to social morality and that the moral truth is always relative to a particular place and time. This differs from expressivism, a view which is that moral statements are neither true nor false in any sense, claiming that moral utterances need to be understood in some non-factual way.[20] For example, one expressivist view holds that saying "polygamy is immoral" is a way of giving a kind of command and should be understood to mean "do not be polygamous!" Commands are not true of false, they put language to work to do something other than making assertions. On this sort of expressivist view (and there are several other versions) moral utterances cannot be factual (that is, they are neither true nor false—they do not have a truth-value); the view that moral utterances can be factual (that is, they are either true or false) is called *moral cognitivism*.

---

20. I will address this kind of moral antirealism in chapter 2.

Let's now summarize the postmodern metaethical positions described so far. Moral antirealists come in two main versions: moral constructivists and moral expressivists. Moral constructivists hold that moral statements are factual, so they are cognitivists, but the truth of a moral statement for them is dependent on the social context implied by the speaker. But on their view there is no moral order, so they are moral antirealists. Moral expressivists hold that moral statements cannot be factual—they are used to do something other than state what is true or false—so expressivists are noncognitivists. But expressivists also deny the moral order, so they are moral antirealists like the constructivists. So moral expressivists and moral constructivists are both moral antirealists, but they differ with regard to how to understand moral utterances. Moral constructivists think that moral statements are true or false, depending on the relevant cultural standards. Moral expressivists think that moral utterances are not about what is true or false, rather they are some other kind of speech act.

In the rest of this chapter we will sharpen the contrast between moral realism and moral antirealism, paying particular attention to constructivism. Moral constructivism is the most plausible form of moral antirealism, and I will try to identify some serious problems with this view. In the next chapter, we will consider expressivism, which I think is demonstrably false. In both chapters I will be arguing for moral realism, since if we can determine that the two main varieties of moral antirealism are problematic and false, then moral realism is the better theory (by *modus tollendo ponens*). I do not think it should be surprising that Plato, Aristotle, and virtually the whole of Western philosophy until the twentieth century got it right.

Constructivism and the Moral Order

Moral constructivism comes in various forms, but what is common to each of them is the idea that the moral standard which a moral judgment employs is nothing more than a construct of some human persons whose beliefs are responsible in some way for the morality that is operating in some time and place. Moral standards are simply the guideposts that each particular society has latched onto as the measure of how a person ought to act. This opinion of how a person ought to act could be changed over time if enough people (or perhaps the right people) altered their opinion. Social constructivists believe that there are different social moralities in different societies. For example, at one time people in the United States generally considered divorce to be immoral, but now that view has changed so that divorce is now something morally permissible in the United States, whereas in the Philippines divorce is still considered morally impermissible. If you ask a social constructivist, "is divorce really morally right or wrong?" he would say something like, "at one time in the United States it was morally wrong, but now it is morally permitted." If you pressed on and asked, "But is it morally right that divorce is morally permitted in the United States?" the constructivist does not believe there is any moral standard by which that question can be answered. For a social constructivist, there is no moral reality behind or beyond or beneath social morality. The moral reality which a moral utterance expresses when it is true is not fixed for all times and all places, but varies depending on what is accepted and approved in society at the time. Of course, some of the precepts in a social morality are the basis for the laws which are enacted in a society.

Some constructivists take the view that such social conventions are neither natural nor accidental, but the intentional, selected rules produced by some people in a society. For example, Nietzsche thought that morality is no more than one way persons with more power in a society control the people with less power in order to advance their own self-interest. This constructivist view may lead to an *ethics of suspicion* where the rules that people are encouraged to live by are examined to see whose interests they promote.

In contrast to constructivism, the concept of the moral order is that of a moral reality which is not a construct of human persons and is not variable depending on human opinion. The moral order is a standard of conduct that is above and beyond both the approved norms of conduct in a society and the laws of any nation, a moral reality which is binding on every person, every society, and every culture, regardless of the social morality in which they live. If the moral order exists, and if we can know it, then we have the antidote to moral relativism—the postmodern idea that morality varies from place to place and time to time. As stated above, social moralities as such should be of little interest to philosophers; they are the province of sociologists. As a metaethical theory constructivism is of some interest to philosophers, although it does not lead to the moral order but only to a constructed morality, like social morality. Philosophical interest in ethics has traditionally been primarily an interest in normative issues; that is, what is morally right or wrong in the light of the moral order—and this is a light that antirealists cannot see.

We have seen that classical moral theorists believe that the moral order exists and try to *discover* exactly what conduct it requires. In the last century this assumption has come under a relentless attack, to the point where virtually all intellectuals and even the uneducated have come to doubt or deny it. Some surveys show that most Americans, at any rate, do not believe there are any moral absolutes.[21] If you were to ask whether there is a moral order that has precepts that are the same for everyone, regardless of who, when, or where they are, many Americans would express denial or doubt. It seems that most people are constructivists without realizing it. At least insofar as they accept the aphorism "do in Rome as the Romans do" they are (implicit) constructivists, thinking that moral judgments are true or false depending on where one is and what conduct is accepted and approved by the people in that place.

Describing the Moral Order

The moral order is the standard of conduct that applies to every act of any agent, personal or superpersonal.[22] A personal agent is an individual acting on his own; a *superpersonal agent* is not an individual, but an institutional moral agent. When a nation enters into war with another nation, that is not the simple act of an individual, it is the act of a government, and a government is one clear example of a superpersonal agent. Corporations, universities, churches, and other institutions are superpersonal agents. The acts of such agents, like the acts of individual persons, are under the governance of the moral order. And some superpersonal agents have morally permissible possibilities that individual agents typically lack. Thus a moral precept like *a government may execute a justly convicted mass murderer* may be true, while no individual (that isn't acting as the agent of such a government) may do so. The moral status of the conduct of superpersonal agents

---

21. "In two national surveys conducted by Barna Research, one among adults and one among teenagers, people were asked if they believe that there are moral absolutes that are unchanging or that moral truth is relative to the circumstances. By a 3-to-1 margin (64% vs. 22%) adults said truth is always relative to the person and their situation. The perspective was even more lopsided among teenagers, 83% of whom said moral truth depends on the circumstances, and only 6% of whom said moral truth is absolute." Barna Group, "Truth on Feelings."

22. In chapter 5 I give reasons for thinking of the moral order as primarily dealing with human acts.

is primarily a topic for social ethics. The point here is that the moral order is also expressed by moral precepts involving superpersonal agents.

As evidenced above, what we are calling "the moral order" has been a topic of great interest throughout the history of Western thought. But we should say more about this important concept and explain some of the properties that have been attributed to it. The moral order is: objective, universal, knowable, rationally consistent, and transcendent. Let's take a brief look at what each of these mean.

The moral order is *objective*, which is to say that it is not a creation of, nor it is affected by, any human believing, willing, desiring, choice, acting, thinking, sentiment or any other human doing. It is an independent reality and exists whether or not any human person thinks so. In this way it is like the tree outside my window that exists whether or not I am looking at it or thinking about it at all. Because the moral order is objective, it is the proper subject matter of a science, the science of ethics.

The moral order is also *universal*, which means that it is binding on all people in all places at all times. The moral order is universal in two ways. First, it is a standard of conduct for every moral agent there ever was, there is, or there ever will be. Adam, Eve, Buddha, Jesus, as well as your great-great grandchildren are subject to it. Even in an afterlife human moral agents would be bound by it. Second, the truth of judgments based on the moral order does not change over time, place, or circumstance. No act-token that once was morally impermissible can become over time something morally permissible. If it was morally wrong for Brutus to have a hand in the assassination of Julius Caesar in 44 BC, then it is still wrong today.

This universality of the moral order needs to be understood correctly in order to avoid confusion. As already noted, sometimes a person will think that morality is relative to the culture in which someone is acting. In the United States it is morally obligatory that you drive on the right side of the road, while in Kenya people drive on the left side. So to some it may seem what is morally obligatory depends on where you live. In fact, the same moral precept is true in both places: *obeying the rules of the road of the country in which one is driving is morally obligatory*. Since the rules of the road vary from country to country the acts that are morally obligatory will vary. This does not make the moral order relativistic, rather it illustrates that the same moral precept may permit different laws in different places.

Moral Reality

Moral rules[23] may vary from place to place, but moral precepts and principles do not change. Again, imagine there is a positive law in Belize that no person may cut down a tree without a government permit. Suppose Sadis cuts down a tree illegally. What Sadis has done is morally impermissible because *disobeying a positive law (that is not itself morally impermissible) is morally impermissible* is part of the moral order. So cutting down a tree is morally impermissible in Belize, but it may not be in Canada.[24]

The moral order is *knowable*; that is, it is epistemologically accessible and one can know it at least in part. A person may not know all of it or know it well, but in some respects at least, it is knowable. For example, most everyone knows that it is wrong to torture and kill infants. Many of the most heinous morally impermissible acts are rather clear to most people, as are many of the most obvious moral obligations, like keeping promises. There are some less obvious moral judgments, and that is one reason why we need a moral theory. A moral theory makes it easier to make close calls about the moral order with confidence. In chapter 6 I will give an account of how we can know the moral order.

The moral order is also *rationally consistent*. This means that the moral order determines that every act has one and only one moral property, so the moral order is a logically coherent system. No act is both morally impermissible and morally permissible. The moral order may also be reasonable—that non-moral reasons give evidence for what moral property an act has. This last claim will be taken up in chapters 4 and 7.

And finally, the moral order is *transcendent*. Transcendence is related to the universality of the moral order and the general nature of the moral order, such that it cannot be identified with any particular set of positive laws or social norms. Positive laws and social norms are specific, and often legally prohibit certain acts that, when considered by themselves, are actually morally permissible. The flat tax in one country may be 36% of one's income, and that is what one is morally obliged to pay. In another country the flat tax may be 40% of one's income, and then that is what one is morally obliged to pay. Both a 36% and a 40% flat tax, however, are morally permissible in themselves. Normally debates about most of the laws for a nation are between morally permissible options, and the choice between them is

---

23. Cf. chapter 3 for an explanation of moral rules.
24. The possible confusion here has to do with properly describing the act, a topic covered in chapter 3. In the present case, in order to give a complete description of the event act-token, it requires that the law of the nation be included.

a political issue and not a moral one, but there are exceptions. A proposed law that would require all poor pregnant women to undergo an abortion would be not just a political matter but a moral matter. Deciding the tax laws for a particular country, however, typically is not a moral matter but a political one.

So the moral order is objective, universal, knowable, rationally consistent, and transcendent. The differences between it and social morality are striking and important. Yet it is obvious that social moralities exist. The important philosophical issue is whether the moral order exists.

Does the Moral Order Exist?

It is one thing to describe the concept of the moral order, and it is another thing to demonstrate or give evidence that there exists a moral principle and/or moral precepts that are objective, universal, knowable, rationally consistent, and transcendent. How does one go about proving that? One strategy would be to produce it—to lay out a true moral principle and set of moral precepts. And numerous philosophers have attempted to do just that, a list including Aquinas, Immanuel Kant, J. S. Mill, Alan Gewirth, and many others. Of course, if one is a moral antirealist, he denies that it is even possible to produce a true moral theory, just as a staunch atheist does not think one can produce a true doctrine of God. So it is not that the moral antirealists looked closely at these and various other moral theories and came to the conclusion that they are mistaken. Moral antirealists are of the opinion that the whole enterprise of trying to identify the moral order is misguided since there is nothing for it to identify. For hundreds, even thousands of years, the only metaethical theory was the classical view. Today, however, the situation is completely changed so that the current academically respectable view is moral antirealism. This dramatic change in the climate of opinion is so dominant in academia that moral realists are becoming an endangered species. So it is worth considering a few of the historical changes that have contributed to the current state of affairs.

Four Changes that Helped to Change the Climate of Opinion

While there are numerous factors that contribute to any change in the climate of opinion, we can identify four factors that have played a significant role in displacing moral realism with moral antirealism. A brief survey of these, in no particular order, will help us understand how this change has come about.

One early factor that began to change the climate of opinion has been the growth and influence of romanticism. "[Romanticism is] a rejection of the precepts of order, calm, harmony, balance, idealization, and rationality that typified Classicism in general and late 18th-century Neoclassicism in particular. It was also to some extent a reaction against the Enlightenment and against 18th-century rationalism and physical materialism in general. Romanticism emphasized the individual, the subjective, the irrational, the imaginative, the personal, the spontaneous, the emotional, the visionary, and the transcendental."[25] Romanticism was a revolt against all external sources of intellectual and moral constraint. The aim was to free the individual to express himself or herself guided only by feelings and personal opinion. It was the intellectual foundation for the French revolution. Jean-Jacques Rousseau was one leading proponent of romanticism, and he certainly followed his heart—he had five children with his servant mistress and abandoned them all. The romanticist idea that personal feelings and desires are the final determinants of what to do erodes interest in the moral precepts that would constrain such conduct.

Another change affecting the climate of opinion was the success of the empirical sciences in the modern and postmodern eras. Science relies on empirical evidence, and this has led some to the view that only scientific learning is truly rational. Traditional moral theories, on the other hand, are not scientific in this way. You cannot visually see or otherwise empirically detect that some act is morally impermissible or morally obligatory. So moral theorizing has been discounted as a possible field of knowledge.[26] In the last 100 years or so this "scientific" viewpoint has been energized by evolutionary theory, which in its atheist versions undercuts the uniqueness of humanity—a pivotal building block for the moral order. Thus, the climate of opinion has become increasingly inhospitable to moral realism.

A third change has encouraged moral antirealism—the loss of Christian faith in the West. As recently as 200 years ago almost all professors teaching in American universities were Christians. A belief in moral realism is the reasonable view for Christians since they believe that human

---

25 Scarfe, "Romanticism."

26. In chapter 6, I will address this epistemological mindset and try to demonstrate that we can truly know a lot about morality (and art). My present purpose, however, is to give historical reasons why moral realism has come under attack.

persons are created in the image of God and share a unique human nature. As the creator of human beings, God establishes the moral order, and all human beings ought to conform their lives to this order. Religion in general, and Christianity in particular, emphasizes that God attends to the affairs of people and has a standard of conduct by which people should act. Today the situation is radically changed. Not only are most professors not Christians, there is hostility at many schools toward Christianity. For many academics, atheistic evolutionary theory has undercut faith in the value of humanity and in the God who created humanity.[27] As fewer professors and other intellectuals are religious, they express increased doubt, suspicion, and even hostility toward moral realism.[28]

One additional reason for the change in the climate of opinion about moral realism is more of a technological advance than an intellectual change—increased globalization. A century ago, when most people lived only in their own communities, they were not as aware of other cultures and ways of life. They were not exposed to alternative sets of mores. Today, however, through travel, business, and media, people learn about the wide variety of social moralities. They discover that there are alternative ways to eat, date, govern, etc. When people are more isolated, they tend to think the only way to do things is the way they do them, and so they absolutize their own view as the correct ones. This happens with respect to morality as well. If a person grows up in a closed environment with the view, for example, that interracial marriage is morally impermissible, one is likely to think this is the correct view and that everyone shares it. However, as persons encounter a diversity of social moralities they become less convinced of moral absolutes. People see that different societies have different rules, and so they conclude that there are no fixed moral truths. (But of course, as described above, the way in which societies conform to the moral order can vary from one society to another.)

These four developments: the rise of romanticism, the epistemological tilt toward empiricism, the decline in Christian belief, and increased globalization, are some of the primary factors in radically changing the climate of opinion in Western culture regarding the existence of the moral order. Moral realism is caught in a climate of opinion maelstrom. Today

---

27. Evolution, as a theory of change and development, is not incompatible with Christianity, except in those versions of it that are based on unguided and random change. Cf. Plantinga, *Conflict*.

28. Christianity (and other religious faiths) tend to support moral realism, but one need not be religious to be a moral realist.

one is often regarded with suspicion for even suggesting that some things are morally obligatory, and one can be condemned for saying something is morally wrong. If the moral order is not real, then there is no objective standard for judging others, and it is a mistake to think anything or anyone is morally wrong in any trans-cultural sense.

Problems with Moral Antirealism

Although a person may deny that there are any moral precepts that are objective and universal, he finds numerous occasions to scold, criticize, and condemn others who don't conform to his idea of what you should believe or say or do. As Phillip Yancey says, "[T]he new moralists first proclaim that morality is capricious, maybe even a joke, then proceed to use moral categories to condemn their opponents. These new high priests lecture us solemnly about multiculturalism, gender equality, homophobia, and environmental degradation, all the while ignoring the fact that they have systematically destroyed any basis for judging such behavior right or wrong. The emperor so quick to discourse about fashion happens to be stark naked."[29]

The specific issues that Yancey identifies are not the point here. The point is that it is very difficult to consistently avoid speaking in terms of moral properties that are not based on merely cultural beliefs. And it isn't that a moral antirealist thinks the condemnation of, say, racism, is restricted within one culture or even civilization. It isn't a claim limited to one's social morality. No, the claim is that racism is morally wrong in any culture. Moral *realists* have no struggle in making such claims, but those who deny the moral order have a practical dilemma of wanting to make universal moral judgments but without the ontology that would make sense of such assertions. Their problem is not resolved by coming up with an alternative moral hermeneutic because many moral antirealists want to say that racism *really* is wrong—they don't simply mean that that's how they feel about it, nor do they mean to be simply expressing themselves. The problem of the moral antirealist calls to mind what Winston Churchill said, "The truth is incontrovertible, malice may attack it, ignorance may deride it, but in the end, there it is."[30] The irrepressible tendency to make moral judgments is one reason for believing that there is a moral order.

29. Yancey, "Nietzsche," 14.
30. Churchill, "Truth."

But the underlying problem for moral antirealists is not that their view delegitimizes their moral speech, it is that their view denies there are any universal moral truths. Without a moral order it isn't just that one cannot say that some act is morally wrong, it is that no act really can be morally wrong. At most any wrong is merely a violation of some social morality, a violation of some cultural mores. Without a moral order there are no intrinsic human rights, only whatever rights that are conferred socially. If there are any human rights, then everyone has moral obligations to respect these and we have a moral order; if there are no human rights, then in a sufficiently corrupt society, evil may be thought good. Without a moral order as the standard for conduct, every person and every society is equally good and equally bad because, although there may be cultural rules, there is no way to justify one set of rules as proper or correct. Thus there are no justifiable rules for properly structuring personal life, social interactions, or international relations. In this situation, what is *actually* good and right does not exist, and so cannot matter. The final organizing force for human life would be nothing but coercion executing the will of the person who holds power. If individuals and nations were ordered only by the law that might makes right, the stronger would do what they want and the weaker would be of little account. What arguments can the weak muster to dissuade the powerful? That some acts are unjust? Unfair? To what can they appeal? Without the moral order, no pleading about justice or fairness has any actual weight—these gain their gravitas by referencing the moral order. Without any moral order, we may as well appeal to Zeus or to the rules of Middle Earth. Without the moral order, we would be like animals. In fact, we would be worse off than animals, because we are far more capable of evil calculations. Lions cannot herd victims into boxcars and ship them off to Auschwitz. By denying the moral order each of us becomes an unrestricted free agent without justification for judging our own conduct or the conduct of others. Not only would we not know right from wrong, there would not be any true right or wrong.

It is not a counter-argument to say that even with the moral order there is plenty of barbarism. It's true, I suppose, that the Nazis believed in a moral order and still engaged in moral atrocities. But the Nazis either misunderstood what the moral order required or lacked the will to follow it. Either way, their wrongful conduct is no reason to think the moral order does not exist; it is a reason to try to understand what it requires and follow it. In fact—and this is telling—without a moral order we could not know that what the Nazis did was wrong.

The tragic consequences of moral antirealism should lead anyone to hope that the moral order exists, but it does not establish it. What it does show is that it is important that most people believe that it exists. If people simply believe there is a higher law—a morality—then they may, to some extent, try to live in a way somewhat consistent with it. If a person thinks there is a moral order, then arguments that appeal to it may have some weight with her. Believing that there is a moral order gives meaning to a person's moral utterances, and sets limits on what a person thinks is morally right.

Conclusion

We started by wondering with Outka and Reeder if there was any hope for a common morality. Their quest was for "common morality" that was both universal and justifiable. But "universal" is ambiguous; it can be understood either positively or normatively. The prospects for establishing a universal morality in the positive sense are dim at best. Of more interest is the hope to identify a universal morality in the normative sense—the moral order.

There may not be any reasons sufficient to persuade someone that there is a moral order, but it takes a lot of effort *not* to believe it exists. One keeps running up against the tendency to say and think that some things really are right and good and other things really are wrong and bad. Still, some people will expend that considerable effort, in spite of the miserable implications that such a view has for humanity—where selfishness, slander, murder, greed, and betrayal are not really wrong but merely alternative lifestyle choices or contrary to social conventions.

It is time again for moral theorists to return to the issues associated with the moral order: how can we identify what is morally impermissible, morally obligatory, and morally permissible? How can we know what is morally good or morally bad? But before we can turn our attention to the moral order, we need to consider moral realism's chief rival in metaethical circles—expressivism. If I can show that expressivism is untenable, then the case for moral realism becomes that much stronger. That is the task of the next chapter.

2

Moral Language

The majority of Western philosophers since Socrates have assumed that moral judgments were bearers of truth value. Each moral statement was either true or false, and moral theories helped one to know which judgments were true and which were false. As I have noted, early in the twentieth century this assumption came under fire. One accelerant to this was a philosophical version of radical empiricism called *verificationism*, which was inspired in large part by the success of the physical sciences.

Verificationism is a view of meaning, and, roughly speaking, it maintains that contingent statements[1] which cannot be empirically verified are meaningless; that is, if a contingent statement cannot be determined to be true or false using the five senses, then it is meaningless. So a statement like "John is a good person" is meaningless, as is "God loves me" or even "My mother loves me." Since moral statements do not seem to be verifiable in this way, they must be meaningless and neither true nor false. Unfortunately for the verificationists, their theory of meaning *if it cannot be determined whether a contingent statement is true or false solely by empirical means, then it is meaningless* is itself a contingent claim, and it is not able to be verified through empirical means. Thus verificationism was hoist on its own petard and has long been discredited. But the view of moral judgments that it helped to spawn—that moral judgments are neither true nor false—has had a long run through the twentieth century. It spurred a largely fruitless enterprise we can call *moral hermeneutics*. The key questions of

---

1. A contingent statement is one which is possibly true—neither necessarily true, like two plus two is four, nor necessarily false, like one plus one is three.

moral hermeneutics include: if moral statements cannot express truth, how should we understand them and what is their function or purpose?

These questions have occupied moral philosophers throughout much of the twentieth century and the first decade of the twenty-first. This attention has given rise to a variety of theories about moral language such as *emotivism* (the view that moral judgments are no more than expressions of emotion) and *prescriptivism* (the view that moral judgments are to be understood as expressions like prescriptions or proscriptions). Each of these is a version of *expressivism* (any view where moral judgments express something other than facts.) The view that moral judgments are neither true nor false is called *noncognitivism*, the view that grounds each version of expressivism. The alternative view—that moral judgments are either true or false, i.e., that they bear a truth value—is called *cognitivism*. Either cognitivism or noncognitivism is true, and in this chapter I will argue for cognitivism. The classical tradition was correct; the focus on moral hermeneutics has been minimally instructive, a long detour into an intellectual cul-de-sac.

My argument has two parts. First, I will examine some arguments that noncognitivists have used against cognitivism and show that they completely miss the mark. For this I will use some of the work of William K. Frankena, a careful philosopher who was sympathetic to noncognitivism and one who explains clearly the main arguments against cognitivism. If I am successful in showing the arguments used against cognitivism are unsound it will advance the case for cognitivism—the view that moral judgments are either true or false. But it would not prove that cognitivism is true, however, as it would still be possible that there are other arguments for or against cognitivism. Thus, in the second part of this chapter I explain three problems for noncognitivism that make it untenable.

Arguments against Cognitivism

William K. Frankena taught philosophy at the University of Michigan for 41 years, retiring in 1978. He published many scholarly articles, and his little textbook *Ethics* was widely used. He favored noncognitivism and was a rather early American entrant in the field of moral hermeneutics. Frankena distinguishes three kinds of noncognitivist moral hermeneutics.[2] The most extreme kind of, according to Frankena, is A. J. Ayer's *emotivism*. A. J. Ayer's view was that moral judgments are merely expressions of emotion with no rational component and so are not of theoretical interest. Frankena identifies a second kind of noncognitivism with the view of C. L. Stevenson, which he considers a less extreme version of emotivism. Frankena says that Stevenson's view is that moral judgments express one's attitude toward something. According to Stevenson, such "moral" attitudes on which these judgments are made are frequently based on beliefs. These underlying beliefs can be reasoned about and thus, to some extent, justify one attitude as more reasonable than another. (I will leave it to the reader to try to understand what the relationship could be between a belief which is either true or false and the expression of an attitude which is neither. It cannot be a *logical* relation.) A third kind of noncognitivism is what Frankena considers the least extreme version. This is the view that moral judgments function as recommendations or prescriptions and is called *prescriptivism*. Since a prescription can be wise or foolish, helpful or harmful, this way of taking moral judgments appears to have a rational basis. If your boss tells you to "Shut the door," what he says has meaning, and can be a good or bad command, but it is not true or false. Frankena aligns his own view with this third kind of noncognitivism.

Frankena identifies only two kinds of cognitivism: definism and intuitionism.[3] Definism is the view of moral theories that is based on a moral predicate being synonymous with a non-moral predicate. For a definist utilitarian, "is morally impermissible" is synonymous with "does not produce the greatest net utility." The definist's claim is then that two synonymous predicates refer to the very same property. In contrast to definism, intuitionism is based not on the meaning of predicates but on an intuition that some specified moral property is coextensive with some non-moral property. (When two properties are coextensive, anything that has one property has the other as well. So *has shape* and *has weight* are coextensive, since nothing can have a shape without having a weight or vice versa.) One version of intuitionism holds that *is morally obligatory* and *is commanded*

---

2. Frankena, *Ethics*, 105–7.
3. Ibid., 98.

by God are coextensive; thus any act that has one of these properties also has the other.[4]

Frankena identifies three main arguments used by noncognitivists against cognitivism.[5] The first is called the Open Question Argument and is aimed at definism. It attempts to show that no moral predicate is synonymous with a non-moral predicate. The other two arguments are against intuitionism; I will call them the No Motivation Argument and the Sensible Question Argument.

Definism and the Open Question Argument

As stated above, definism is the view that a moral predicate is synonymous with some non-moral predicate. In Frankena's words, definism is the view that "ethical terms can be defined in terms of non-ethical ones, and ethical sentences can be translated into metaethical ones of a factual kind."[6] This parallels rather precisely Ayer's account in *Language, Truth and Logic* in which he writes, "What we are interested in is the possibility of reducing the whole sphere of ethical terms to non-ethical terms. We are inquiring whether statements of ethical value can be translated into statements of empirical fact."[7] Definism, according to Frankena and Ayer, is a kind of moral theory that is based on the claimed synonymy of a moral predicate and a non-moral one.

There are two kinds of definism possible. *Naturalism* defines a moral term in terms of sensible properties. For example, the view that the moral predicate "is morally good" means the same as "produces pleasure" is an example of this kind of definism, since pleasure is an empirically discernible property. *Non-naturalism* is a theory in which a moral predicate is claimed to be synonymous with a "metaphysical" predicate, for example, the view that "is morally obligatory" is synonymous with "is God's will."

Ayer, for one, has no sympathy for non-natural or "metaphysical" predicates, and thus does not even consider non-naturalism an option. Instead, he divides naturalism into two kinds. One kind of naturalism Ayer

---

4. On this version of intuitionism the corresponding propositions, *p is morally obligatory* and *p is commanded by God*, are materially equivalent, that is, they always have the same truth value.

5. Frankena, *Ethics*, 97.

6. Ibid., 98.

7. Ayer, *Language*, 104.

calls *subjectivism*, which Ayer understands as any claim that a moral predicate is synonymous with feelings of approval or disapproval. When Jonathan says, "Lying is morally wrong" what he is saying is synonymous with "I, Jonathan, have feelings of disapproval toward lying." The other kind of definism Ayer countenances is *utilitarianism*, which he says is the attempt to define "the rightness of actions, and the goodness of ends, in terms of the pleasure, or happiness, or satisfactions, to which they give rise."[8] If we take pleasure as a case in point, "Lying is morally wrong" would be synonymous with "Lying does not produce the greatest net pleasure." The Open Question Argument must be an impressive argument if it is to undermine all these various views. It certainly has been a popular argument. G. E. Moore, A. J. Ayer, and W. Frankena all employ it. Much more recently, John E. Hare has made use of it.[9] Many others have assumed its soundness in criticizing metaethical views or in developing them.

Frankena gives this explanation of the Open Question Argument.

> Suppose that a definist holds that "good" or "right" means "having the property P," for example, "being desired" or "being conducive to the greatest general happiness." Then, the argument is that we may agree that something has P, and yet ask significantly, But is it good?" or "Is it right?" That is, we cam sensibly say, "This has P, but is it good (or right)?" But if the proposed definition were correct, then we could say this sensibly for it would be equivalent to saying, "This has P, but has it P?" which would be silly. Likewise one can say, "This has P but it is not good (or right)," without contradicting oneself, which could not be the case if the definition were correct. Therefore the definition cannot be correct.[10]

So the argument is intended to show that a moral predicate and a nonmoral predicate cannot be synonymous. The way this is demonstrated is as follows: if one predicate is substituted for the other in a question, one of the questions has an obvious answer, the other results is an open question. (An "open question" is one whose answer is still in doubt.) If two predicates are synonymous, then when either one is substituted for the other in a question the "openness" of the question should not change. When the openness of

---

8. Ibid., 104.

9. Hare, *God's Call*, 36. "I think there is a version of Moore's Open Question Argument that still applies."

10. Frankena, *Ethics*, 104.

the question does change, the conclusion is that the two predicates are not synonymous.

Consider a definist who holds that "is morally obligatory" is synonymous with "is commanded by God." The question "This is morally obligatory, but is it morally obligatory?" is not an open question, but if you make a substitution the question becomes "This is commanded by God, but is it morally obligatory?" which is an open question. Since the first question is not an open question and the second is, the conclusion is that "is morally obligatory" is not synonymous with "is commanded by God."

At first glance it seems that the Open Question Argument is flawed. As a parallel instance, consider the Latin word *mater* and the English word *mother*. These two terms are synonymous, but suppose Lance does not know any Latin and is in his first day of Latin class. If his Latin teacher asks him "is your mother your mother?" The answer is obvious; this is not an open question for Lance (or for anyone), but suppose the teacher asks him "is your mother your *mater*?" The answer to this question is not obvious to Lance, for him it is an open question. If a person does not know that two terms are synonymous, and if he knows the meaning of one of them, then a question framed with one term will be open, and the same question using the synonymous term is not open. At most the Open Question Argument shows that what is proposed as a technical explanation/definition of a moral term is not the common understanding. This the definist can admit without concern because it fails to refute what he is proposing. The definist is attempting to explain what we might call a deeper truth about moral reality, for example, that what is morally good is really what benefits most people.

The argument is based on a commonly understood sense of the predicates involved, but the definist is trying to teach and explain a deeper meaning of the moral predicate, one which is not commonly understood.[11] For example, he may be saying that the propositions *p is God's will* and *p is morally good* are materially equivalent.[12] If and when one fully accepts this,

---

11. Frankena suggests something like this is a reply that is available to the definist. "He may argue that the meaning of words like "good" and "right" in ordinary use is very unclear, so that when a clarifying definition of one of them is offered, it is almost certain not to retain all of what we vaguely associate with the term. Thus, the substitute cannot seem to be entirely the same as the original, and yet may turn out to be an acceptable definition." Frankena, *Ethics*, 105.

12. The usual relationship claimed to exist between a moral proposition and a non-moral one is more than material equivalence, as is explained in chapter 4. Two

the propositions *p is God's will* and *p is morally good* will be equally self-evident to him, and the question "p is God's will, but is p morally good?" is not an open question.

Consider another case, one from the physical sciences. The two predicates "is water" and "is H2O" in one sense *mean* the same thing in that they refer to the same substance. Imagine a child that does not know that water is H2O. If the child is asked, "this is water, but is it water?" the answer is obvious; it would not be an open question to even a five year old. But "this is water, is it H2O?" would be an open question. So the Open Question Argument applied to these terms leads to the conclusion that they do not mean the same thing. Although "is water" and "is H2O" refer to the same substance, in fact, these two statements are not synonymous; they do not have the same semantic meaning. They refer to the same substance—which is the point that scientists want to make. A scientist does not engage in an investigation into the common meaning of the words used to refer to the things she's investigating. She considers the nature of the things themselves. And it is a mistake to think that moralists are not like scientists in this respect. They are not giving a commonly understood linguistic meaning of a moral predicate, but attempting to explain moral reality. A moral philosopher, even a definist, is not a philologist, nor linguist, nor a lexicographer, and it is an error to think he is proposing a theory that is about or based on the commonly understood meanings of words.

Intuitionism and the Arguments against It

The two arguments used against intuitionism are the Sensible Question Argument and the No Motivation Argument. Frankena describes moral intuitionism: "According to this view, as for the definists, ethical judgments are true or false; but they are not factual and cannot be justified by empirical observation or metaphysical reasoning. The basic ones, particular or general, are self-evident and can only be known by intuition; this follows, it is maintained, from the fact that the properties involved are simple and non-natural."[13] On the intuitionist account, we know moral truths through a human faculty called *intuition*. This faculty does not yield empirical truth, nor is it dependent on such truths. But it is a rational faculty. Moreover, it

---

propositions are materially equivalent when they always have the same truth value, so if one is true so is the other one.

13. Frankena, *Ethics*, 103.

can be more developed and more accurate in some people than in others, like the sense of smell or hearing. When a person who has a reliable intuition grasps a situation she is often able to recognize the moral properties of the possible acts in the situation. Moral properties are self-evident to such a person with something like the same kind of clarity as identifying a gunshot is to a person with hearing.[14] In our present context, what is important is that intuitionism holds that a moral judgment involves attributing a moral property to something, and such attributions can be true or false.

G. E. Moore was an intuitionist. In *Principia Ethica* he writes, "'[G]ood' is a simple notion, just as 'yellow' is a simple notion; that, just as you cannot, by any manner of means, explain to anyone who does not already know it, what yellow is, so you cannot explain what good is."[15] Moral properties are simple, unanalyzable, and *sui generis*; there is no way of referring to them without using moral terms. Moore used a version of the Open Question Argument against any view that claims a moral predicate and a non-moral predicate are synonymous. Intuitionism is the view that there is moral reality, which is irreducibly real, and that moral statements are the attribution of real moral properties. On this view, moral statements express propositions and are either true or false, so intuitionists are moral realists and cognitivists.

In what follows I will consider first the Sensible Question Argument, and then the No Motivation Argument, both leveled against intuitionism. I will show that the arguments are unsuccessful as refutations of intuitionism.

The Sensible Question Argument

The Sensible Question Argument in some ways is similar to the Open Question Argument and can be dealt with summarily. The argument starts by supposing that some act A has the property of being morally obligatory. If you then ask "Act A is morally obligatory, but why should a person do A?" you have asked a sensible question. But if "A is morally obligatory" means "A is something a person should do" and we substitute it in the question, we do not get a sensible question: "Why should a person do what a person should do?" Thus "act A is morally obligatory" and "a person should do A" do not mean the same thing. The conclusion drawn is that moral judgments, like *a person should do A* mean something different than attributing

14. Some of these issues regarding moral epistemology will be taken up in chapter 6.
15. Moore, *Principia Ethica*, 7.

a moral property to act A.[16] This argument tries to show that attributing a moral property to an act is not equivalent to judging that the act should be done (or should be avoided). Those who employ the argument are trying to make the case that a moral judgment implies some action (or inaction), whereas attributing a property is passive in comparison.[17]

But this understanding is mistaken. In normal logical analysis to say "a person should do act A" is also to attribute a property. It is to say "Act A has the property of being such that a person should do it." So if attributing a property is somehow too passive, saying what a person should do is also passive. Moreover, saying "Act A is morally obligatory" is to say "Act A has the property such that a person should do it." Thus "being an act such that a person should do it" and "being morally obligatory" both attribute a property to act A, and in fact express the same property. If the Sensible Question arguer cannot see that a morally obligatory act is one that a person should do, that betrays a remarkable linguistic and/or moral blindness.

The No-Motivation Argument

The second argument addressed against intuitionism, which comes from Hume,[18] is what we can call the No Motivation Argument. The argument, which is not presented clearly by either Hume or Frankena, seems to have the following premises:

16. In Frankena's account, the argument is: "Let us suppose, it is said, that there are such brave non-natural and indefinable properties as the intuitionists talk about. Let us also suppose that act A has one of these properties, P. Then one can admit that A has P and still sensibly ask, "But why should I do A?" One could not do this if "I should do A" means "A has P"; hence it does not mean "A has P" as the intuitionists think." Clearly Frankena intends "P" as a variable standing for some moral property. Frankena, *Ethics*, 104.

17. Frankena writes, "Even after studying them I find myself doubting that any pure definist theory, whether naturalistic or metaphysical, can be regarded as adequate as an account of what we do mean. For such a theory holds that an ethical judgment simply is an assertion of a fact—that ethical terms constitute merely an alternative vocabulary for reporting facts. It may be that they should be reinterpreted so that this is the case. In actual usage, however, this seems clearly not to be so. When we are making merely factual assertions we are not thereby taking any pro or con attitude toward what we are talking about; we are not recommending it, prescribing it, or anything of the sort. But when we make an ethical judgment we are not neutral in this way; it would seem paradoxical if one were to say "X is good" or "Y is right" but be absolutely indifferent to its being sought or done by himself or anyone else." Ibid., 101.

18. Hume, *Treatise*, 455–70.

Moral Language

(1) A moral judgment p about an act A must provide a motive for anyone who accepts p to either do A or refrain from doing A.

More simply, and less precisely, the idea is that moral judgments must motivate the persons who accept them. Thus if Jack accepts that murder is morally wrong, then Jack must be motivated to refrain from committing any murder.

(2) If a judgment p ascribes a moral property to some act A, then one could accept p and not be provided with a motive to either do A or refrain from doing A.

So the argument is that if moral beliefs are factual, that is, either true or false, then they may not provide a motivation for a person who holds the belief to do or avoid any particular act. But, the argument maker contends, moral beliefs must always be motivating. The conclusion drawn from the No Motivation Argument is that moral beliefs are not factual. Facts about acts do not always motivate persons. From (1) and (2) it follows that moral judgments are not the ascriptions of moral properties to acts.

Understanding this argument depends on how one understands the rather vague idea of a motive. There are, I think, two different senses of "motive" which may be operating in this argument. According to one, a motive is a kind of desire, so that providing a motive is to generate a desire. According to the other, a motive is a reason, in which case providing a motive to do or refrain from an act is to provide a reason for doing or refraining from the act. Frankena takes the argument in a way which suggests that he understands "providing a motive" as "providing a desire." One can see this in his criticism of the argument when Frankena suggests that the intuitionist could claim that accepting that some act A has some property P does produce a psychological pro-attitude regarding the performing of A.[19] Such a "pro-attitude" seems more akin to a desire than to a reason. So the argument probably ought to be understood as taking "a motive to do A or refrain from doing A" as meaning "I desire to do A or refrain from doing A." Yet this will not matter as I will show that the argument is not persuasive on either reading. For the sake of argument we can overlook these objections and consider the No Motivation Argument in the case where the denotation of "A" is restricted to act-types.[20] In order to do this

---

19. Frankena, *Ethics*, 107.

20. In chapter 3 I will explain what an act-type is more fully, for now it is enough to know that it refers to a kind of act rather than a particular instance of an act. So "murder" is an act-type, and the assassination of John F. Kennedy is not an act-type, but an instance

most efficiently, however, it is advantageous to consider the two ways of interpreting the argument separately.

The No Motivation Argument: No Reason

First consider the argument where "motive" is understood in the sense of "reason." On this interpretation, the intuitionist can affirm (1). The problem for the intuitionist would be with (2). Using "a reason" for "a motive" (2) becomes

(2a) If a judgment s ascribes a moral property to some act-type A, then one could accept s and not be provided with a reason to either do or refrain from doing acts of type A.

Consider, for example, *s* is the moral precept *Adultery is morally wrong*. Further, assume some person, Sam, accepts s. Is it possible that Sam has no reason to refrain from acts of adultery? Suppose Sam carefully avoids being tempted to commit adultery and someone asks him why he does so. Would not his reply "Adultery is morally wrong" count as the reason why he acts the way he does? Of course the interlocutor could go on to ask Sam "How do you know that adultery is wrong?" or "Why is adultery wrong?" But these additional questions are not indications that Sam's answer to the original question did not constitute a *reason*. The additional questions are inquiries into the reasons for Sam's acceptance of the moral judgment, not inquiries into why Sam acts the way he does. The reason for his behavior is his belief that adultery is morally wrong.

But now suppose Rob says he accepts that adultery is morally wrong but commits serial adulteries. Rob's wife asks him, "Don't you know that adultery is morally wrong?" and Rob replies, "Sure." She says, "So why do you keep doing it?" This is a good question because once a person accepts that adultery is morally wrong he has a reason to stop doing it. There is something odd in thinking that some act is morally wrong and then doing it, or in thinking that some act is morally obligatory and then avoiding it. The oddness arises because thinking something is morally wrong (or morally obligatory) does give you a reason to avoid it (or do it). So holding to a moral precept does give a person a reason to act or refrain from acting. Of course, a person may ignore, override, or not even be aware of the reason,

---

of one.

Moral Language

and so act unreasonably. That we sometimes act unreasonably is not because the precept is not true, it is because we often act badly.

It is hard to see what view of reasons supports the No Motivation arguer in claiming that (2a) is true. Perhaps the No Motivation arguer thinks it is true because he is committed to the view that moral precepts are neither true nor false; further, he may hold that only facts can serve as reasons, so that moral precepts cannot serve as reasons. But if this is the support for (2a) the intuitionist clearly will reject it. For intuitionism holds that moral precepts are either factual or not and that moral precepts do provide reasons for acting one way rather than another. Whether a moral judgment is a factual claim is precisely the issue. Insofar as this form of the No Motivation Argument requires that one assume that moral judgments are not factual claims, it begs the question. So on this reading, the No Motivation Argument fails.

No Motivation Argument: No Desire

Now consider the argument taking "a desire" for "a motive." Then (2) becomes

(2b) If a judgment s ascribes a moral property to some act-type A, then one could accept s and not be provided with a desire to either do or refrain from doing acts of type A.

The cognitivist can affirm that (2b) is true. It is possible that a person could accept that some act is morally wrong and have no desire to avoid it, or that some act is morally obligatory and fail to have a desire to do it. It is even possible for a person to be calloused and perverse so that he accepts that some act has the property of being morally wrong and that gives him the desire to do it. The truth is that the desires that we have are not necessarily consonant with our moral views. Maybe it is true that most people are decent enough that desires are linked appropriately to moral views. Perhaps for most people holding that some act is wrong often does generate at least some kind of desire to refrain from doing it. Even so, the fact is that all too often these desires are overruled by stronger and contrary desires. So John knows that lying is morally wrong, but he's in trouble and the only way out is to deny what he did. His desire to avoid responsibility is to lie. Not only is it possible that accepting a moral precept generates a contrary desire, or an easily dismissed or ignored desire, it is possible that it generates no desire at all. No doubt you accept the moral precept *The murder of political enemies by those in political power is morally wrong*. Does this give you any desire to act or refrain from acting? Unless you are or intend to be in political power this precept fails to produce any desire in most people. This shows why the cognitivist can accept (2b).

The problem with the argument on this reading comes with (1) which, when we substitute "a desire" for "a motive," becomes

(1b) A moral judgment q about an act-type A must provide a desire for anyone who accepts q to either do acts or refrain from acts of type A.

It is hard to see why the cognitivist should accept (1b). If there is no necessary connection between one's moral views and one's desires, then (1b) is false. An even greater problem is why the No Motivation arguer would consider (1b) true. Consider the imperativist, for example, who holds that moral judgments are not factual claims but a kind of polite command. How is it that one who accepts such a polite command thereby must have a desire to do what is commanded? Suppose I accept the command "Do not commit adultery!" (What does it mean to accept a command anyway? Perhaps I simply recognize that the person giving the command has the right to do so.) Does it follow that obeying the command is something I must desire? Perhaps accepting a command means one thinks the command is useful or appropriate, but that does not imply that one thereby desires to obey it. Presumably one could avoid desiring what one considers useful or appropriate. Our moral beliefs and our desires are not linked nearly so closely as to make this reading of the No Motivation Argument successful.

I have tried to show that the arguments that have been aimed at discrediting cognitivism are weak. Neither the Open Question Argument, nor the Sensible Question Argument, nor the No Motivation Argument provides a case for thinking that moral judgments cannot be true or false.

The pursuit of moral hermeneutics in the twentieth century has been largely a waste of intellectual energy. Yet it has had two minor philosophic benefits. First, it has contributed to the philosophy of language and made all moralists sensitive to the fact that moral language is frequently used to do things in addition to describing. Second and more important, it has reaffirmed the Aristotelian view that moral philosophy is a practical science and has implications not only for what one believes but frequently for what one does. But one can enjoy both of these benefits and remain a cognitivist.

Three Problems with Noncognitivism

First Problem: Delimiting Moral Judgments

Many contemporary moralists, like John E. Hare, continue with moral hermeneutics. Hare calls himself a prescriptive realist, the prescriptive part of which he describes as "like the other forms of expressivism in that it insists on the prescriptive character of moral judgment."[21] We shall now take a closer look at what noncognitivists call moral judgments.

So far I have conceded without comment the noncognitivist's assumption (usually implicit) that what counts as a moral judgment is a moral precept. A moral precept is a proposition in which a moral predicate is linked not to a specific act, but to a kind of act—an act-type. So in the statement "adultery is morally wrong" the subject, adultery, refers to *a kind* of specific act. Moral precepts use kinds of acts (called "act-types") rather than specific acts (called "act-tokens"). (The next chapter on moral judgments deals with this in greater detail.) One can make moral judgments that use act-types or act-tokens. Moral judgments that link an act-token to a moral predicate will be called *particular moral judgments*. Now let's consider whether expressivism is plausible by considering some particular moral judgments. Consider

(1) Assassinating Abraham Lincoln was morally wrong.

Until now we have only considered moral precepts to give the No Motivation arguer his best case. But if we look at particular moral judgments, the moral hermeneutics of many varieties of expressivism are pathetically weak. Clearly one could affirm (1) and not be prescribing anything to anyone, not be endorsing anything, and not have any reason or desire or motive to refrain from assassinating Abraham Lincoln. The fact that the act being morally evaluated is in the past squashes both the reasons and the desires to refrain from it. Such particular moral judgments are not trivial; they make up a great percentage of the moral judgments that people make. Consider "Bob shouldn't have lied to his wife" or "Barb's abandoning her son is morally wrong." Judgments about the morality of act-tokens already done are an important part of our moral repertoire. Do noncognitivists

---

21. Hare, *God's Call*, 24.

really want us to think that all particular moral judgments, including ones already past, are neither true nor false, but instead prescribe or command?

Now consider a future moral possibility. John's former boss, living in Cameroon, says to his wife over breakfast one morning, "John's divorcing his wife tomorrow is morally wrong." This refers to a future act, and attributes to it a moral property. It does not provide guidance to anyone, nor does it give anyone a reason or a desire to refrain from the act. It is merely John's former boss's report on his view of the moral status of John's impending act. John's former boss may not even disagree with what John is about to do. The wife of John's former boss either agrees with what her husband said or doesn't agree; that is, she either thinks what he said is true or it is not. The point is that even present and future moral judgments may completely lack the kind of orectic function that expressivists attribute to them. They seem to be closer to bare assertions of fact. Of course, in the right context particular moral judgments may give some guidance to action, or reflect the commendation or disdain of the speaker, but this is not always the case.

So it is in the interest of the noncognitivist to maintain that (1) fails to be a moral judgment. But how could he support that view? Is it not a moral judgment when someone says, "For the U.S.A to start the Iraq War was morally wrong"? And to whom does it give any guidance for action, or what does it endorse or not endorse? The one who makes such an utterance clearly is attributing a moral property to an act. Why is this not a moral judgment? Perhaps the noncognitivist would object that particular moral judgments are not what his moral hermeneutics is aimed at. But why not? The noncognitivist engages in moral hermeneutics selecting those moral judgments that are of interest to him, ignoring others, and concludes that his analysis of moral language shows that all moral judgments are endorsing, or motivating, or prescriptive.[22] Excluding particular moral judgments from the analysis of moral statements ignores a whole class of moral judgments that look and act like the stating of facts. Thus the cognitivist is under no rational obligation to accept the results of the expressivist moral hermeneutics based on a selected sample of moral judgments.

---

22. This is reminiscent of the logical positivists, who decided which utterances were meaningful and then determined a criterion that such utterances presumably met. Unfortunately for them, as explained early in this chapter, the statement expressing the criterion itself failed to meet their standard.

Moral Language

Second Problem: Interpreting Moral Precepts

Noncognitivists say that ethics concerns itself with universal and not particular moral judgments. But this does not resolve the problem for noncognitivism. As already noted, moral precepts predicate moral properties to act-types, that is, of all the acts of a kind, acts that meet a specific description. So the moral precept *murder is morally wrong* is a short-hand way of saying that every particular act that is an instance of murder has the property of being morally wrong. The meaning of a moral precept is conceptually linked to the act-tokens that fall under the act-type that the moral precept uses. Thus *telling lies is morally impermissible* is conceptually related to *John's telling a lie yesterday was morally impermissible*. Any hermeneutic that gives an explanation of the moral precept about telling lies conceptually leads to an interpretation of the particular moral judgment involving John's lying. But we have already noted that particular moral judgments are often a problem for expressivist theories. Saying *the assassination of Julius Caesar was morally wrong* does not seem to be prescribing, commending, commanding, or motivating anything. But if the expressivist interprets *assassinations of political leaders is morally impermissible* to prescribe, commend, command, or motivate that something not be done, then would it not be the case that not assassinating Julius Caesar is one of those things prescribed, commended, recommended, or motivated? But such particular moral judgments are not well suited to expressivist hermeneutics. How can one be prescribing, commending, commanding or motivating that one not assassinate of Julius Caesar? The claim seems to be that an expressivist hermeneutic only applies to moral precepts, but fails to make sense for particular moral judgments. So saying, "telling lies is morally wrong" is simply prescribing, commending, commanding, or motivating that people not tell lies without implying that John's lying is not prescribed, commended, commanded, or motivated. This cannot be right. If you take moral utterances to do something other than stating something true or false, consistency requires that the interpretation of a moral precept (involving an act-type) also will work for the particular moral judgments involving the act-tokens that fall under the act-type.

The cognitivist account of the relationship between a moral precept and a particular moral judgment is much more reasonable. A moral precept is true if and only if the moral property it predicates of the act-type is true of all the acts that fall under the act-type. The precept "Working with other students on term papers in school is morally impermissible" is false because

37

not all of the acts that are instances of working with other students on term papers are morally impermissible. In fact, it only requires one act-token that falls under the act-type, but which lacks the moral property attributed in a moral precept, for the precept to be false. Conceptually, moral precepts are linked to particular moral judgments and one cannot successfully give a hermeneutic for moral precepts without attention to particular moral judgments. The cognitivist says that all moral precepts are either true or false, and that the truth conditions for a moral precept depends on the truth of all the particular moral judgments whose act-tokens fall under the act-type of the precept.

Third Problem: Misunderstanding What a Moral Theory Is a Theory Of

Few moralists in the history of the Western tradition base their moral theories on the meaning of words. Moralists are making claims about reality, and naturally enough use language to make their claims. They are not making claims about language. When they make claims about morality that correspond with the actual moral state of affairs, their claims are true. Of course, if someone does not believe there is any moral reality, they are moral antirealists. Such thinkers will not think they can say anything that corresponds with the actual moral state of affairs (except to deny that there is moral reality). As explained in chapter 1, moral noncognitivists are antirealists. And as atheists don't do serious theology, moral antirealists do not propose moral theories—they propose metaethical theories.

Moral noncognitivists find it difficult to abandon using moral language even though on their view it cannot be true or false. So they look for another explanation for moral language and propose theories about moral hermeneutics. Traditional moralists would agree that *murdering children is morally impermissible* is true, but this option is not available to moral antirealists. Thus they propose noncognitivist hermeneutic theories about how to understand that precept. In contrast, moral realists affirm the truth of the precept and seek to articulate a moral theory that provides some explanation for why the precept is true and even how we can know that it is.

Noncognitivists sometimes take traditional moral theories and interpret them as if the moralists who propose them are making a claim about moral language. That is how some moralists have come to be called definists, as if their project was to give a definition of moral terms. Part

Moral Language

of this problem can be laid at the feet of some cognitivists who state their conclusions in a potentially misleading way. They may work to identify the property of, say, *being morally obligatory*, and determine that it is either identical to or necessarily coextensive with the property *being that which produces the most pleasure*. Then they may write misleading things like: "so that's what the moral predicate 'is morally obligatory' really means." What they should say, to be precise, is that the moral predicate *refers* to a property that is either identical to or necessarily coextensive with another property, *being that which produces the most pleasure*. Some of those who read or hear this view take the theorist at his word, and consider whether "is morally obligatory" and "being that which produces the most pleasure" are synonymous. Some of them then employ the Open Question Argument in an attempt to show that the phrases are not synonymous. Yet moralists typically are not giving a theory about the meaning of words, rather they are expressing a view as to the identity of the property or one that is necessarily coextensive with a moral property like *being morally obligatory*.

To see how this goes, consider a rough form of utilitarianism, whose moral principle is *x is morally obligatory if and only if x produces the greatest net benefit of any action available to the agent*. Frankena and Ayer take it that a person holding to such a theory must also hold the view that *x is morally obligatory* and *x produces the greatest net benefit of any action available to the agent* are synonymous. Now one way a moralist could attempt to argue for his moral theory would be to ground it in the synonymy of predicates. But most moralists do not use such an argument. Two predicates can refer to the same property or logically related properties without meaning the same thing, that is, without being synonymous. The expressions "the morning star" and "the evening star" are clearly not synonymous, yet both refer to the planet Venus. The utilitarian claim is not that "is morally obligatory" and "produces the greatest net benefit of any action available to the agent" are synonymous. The claim is that they refer to properties that are necessarily coextensive. It is not the claim that the linguistic expressions are synonymous, nor does it entail such a claim. When the divine command theorist says that "is morally obligatory" means "is commanded by God," the way to understand the claim is that these two predicates refer either to the same property or to two properties that are necessarily coextensive. It is not the claim that the predicates are synonymous. (This point was made earlier in connection with the Open Question Argument.)

We can concede that the Open Question Argument may successfully show that no moral predicates are literally *synonymous* with any non-moral predicates. But this is an argument against straw moralists. This argument assumes some serious moral theorists to be making claims about the meaning of words, as if they are doing no more than making a dictionary entry. Thus they are labeled definists, an appellation given by those who disagree with them. But few classical moralists, if any, are definists. If the Open Question Argument soundly shows that moral terms cannot be defined by non-moral terms, it is of little consequence. Traditional moral theories are not claims about the common meanings of moral terms. A traditional moral theory involves making truth claims about reality. A moral principle provides a means for distinguishing true and false moral judgments. That being the case, both the Open Question Argument and the Sensible Question Argument arise from a significant misunderstanding of what a theory of morality is a theory of.

Conclusion

The arguments that noncognitivists use to disprove cognitivism fail. And noncognitivism as an alternative theory has three big problems: it fails to provide an expressivist moral hermeneutic that is credible for particular moral judgments, it requires that we separate the understanding of moral precepts and the particular moral judgments that fall under it, and it is based on a misunderstanding of what moral theories are theories of. Thus it is my contention that cognitivism is the correct theory: each moral judgment is either true or false, and it is the purpose of a normative moral theory to show and possibly explain which ones are true and which ones are not. Of course, true moral judgments will often inspire, motivate, and encourage moral agents to act well, but the fact that they do so does not detract from their bearing truth.

In the next chapter I will begin to show the logical tools that cognitivist moralists can use as they address traditional and important questions about the moral order.

3

Basic Moral Propositions

In this chapter I will explain the basic moral propositions: particular moral judgments, moral precepts, and morally permissible rules. To understand the basic moral propositions, one must first understand moral properties.

Moral Properties

One of the fundamental notions used by moralists is the idea of a moral property. The seven most commonly used moral properties are *being morally right, being morally wrong, being morally permissible, being morally impermissible, being morally obligatory, being morally good, and being morally bad*.[1] It may seem an unnecessary redundancy to include the term "morally" in each of these property names, but it is important for clarity. There are ways of being right or wrong that are not moral, as, for example, when a child gets the right (or wrong) answer on a math quiz. And there are ways

---

1. In fact, since all of these properties can be defined in terms of each other, from just one moral property all the others can be derived. For example, if we take being morally permissible as the basic moral property, then if an act lacks being morally permissible, it is morally impermissible. And if it is morally impermissible not to do an act, then it is morally obligatory. The derivation of the properties being morally good and being morally bad from being morally permissible is more complicated, but in chapter 5 I will show one way it can be done. One can choose any of these seven commonly used moral properties to define all the others. Once you let in one moral property, you get the whole family.

of being good or bad that are not moral, for example, when a dinner is good or a movie is bad.

Expressing and Referring to Properties and Propositions

First, a note on how I will express and refer to moral properties. When naming a property (but not attributing it to anything, that is, not using or employing it), we will italicize it, following philosophical convention. For example, we may assert that *being morally good* is a self-identical property. (Here the property *being morally good* is named and another property is attributed to it, but *being morally good* is not attributed to anything.) Similarly, when a proposition is mentioned, but not asserted, the same strategy will be followed. For example, *the capital of Michigan is Lansing* is a contingent proposition. Here the italicized proposition is merely mentioned (as an example) and is not being asserted. In each of these cases something is being said about a property or a proposition; the property is not attributed to anything and the named proposition is not asserted. The difference here is a distinction between mentioning or naming something and using or asserting it. To assert something is to claim that it is true. Mentioning or naming something makes no claim about the truth value of the thing mentioned or named. When a moral property or a proposition is merely mentioned or named it is italicized.

Another important distinction is between the sense or meaning of a term and what that refers to. This distinction was used in chapter 2 to see how the noncognitivists often misinterpret what moral theorists are saying. Words that express properties have both sense and reference. That is, the terms have a meaning and they refer to a property. The name of something has a meaning that one can trace etymologically, and it is used to refer to the thing. For example, the name "Hooper" is derived from the occupation of making barrels, but in a specific use it may refer to a person with that name (and whose occupation may have nothing to do with barrels). "The morning star" and "the evening star" are not synonymous phrases (they do not have the same meaning) but each refers to the same planet, Venus.

Now this presents a problem. In ordinary English one will occasionally speak of the meaning of a word or phrase, while intending the referent—which can lead to confusion.[2] Laura says to her daughter Rachel,

---

2. The "meaning" of a term is even more ambiguous than this. Sometimes it is used for what the speaker or writer means, so one could inquire "What did you mean by

Basic Moral Propositions

"When I say "playground," it means the one next to the school." When speaking precisely it helps to distinguish the meaning of a word or phrase and what it refers to. Whenever what is under consideration is the meaning of a word or phrase, and not what it refers to, I will place it in quotation marks. For example, *the phrase "being morally good" is composed of three words.* Here the sentence is being mentioned, not asserted, and the phrase *"being morally good"* is itself the subject, so we use both italics and quotation marks. There is a difference between speaking about a property and speaking about the words that express the property, and this difference is made clear in the way they are presented in this text.

One very commonly used moral expression, "morally right" seems to express the property of *being morally right*. The problem is that the expression "action A is morally right" can be interpreted to mean either that *action A is morally permissible* or that *action A is morally obligatory*. So "it is morally right to pay one's taxes" can mean either that *it is morally permissible to pay one's taxes* (a relatively weak assertion) or that *it is morally obligatory to pay one's taxes* (a much stronger assertion). (The same ambiguity does not plague *being morally wrong* since it only names the property *being morally impermissible*.) Since "being morally right" is ambiguous, it is preferable to avoid using it and instead to use either "being morally permissible" or "being morally obligatory," depending on which property is intended. Also, it is better to use "morally impermissible" rather than "morally wrong" because, even though these unambiguously express the same property, the former term stands in a more obvious relationship to *being morally permissible*.

Another complexity arises in trying to sort out the relationship between *being morally permissible* and *being morally obligatory*. In ordinary English usage, a person who claims an act is morally obligatory is claiming that the act is required. An act that is required, however, is also morally permissible. One could say that a morally obligatory act is morally permissible and more, it is required (obligatory). Logically speaking, an act's being morally obligatory is a special case of its being morally permissible. It would be helpful if we had a term for the moral property of those acts that are morally permissible and not morally obligatory—acts that are morally permissible *simpliciter*. But there is no such term.[3] (We could try to

---

saying that?" In other cases it is used for a meaning that it independent of the speaker or writer, so one could inquire "What does the name 'Habbakuk' mean?"

3. This problem with moral terms and properties is paralleled in metaphysics by the modal terms "possible" and "necessary." In ordinary English a state of affairs that is necessary is, of course, possible. But in technical contexts where modal issues are discussed,

use "morally permissible" in a restricted sense—only to refer to what is permissible but not obligatory—but this is not what "permissible" means.) Because of this overlap between the extension of the property of *being morally obligatory* and *being morally permissible*, it is usually clearest to express moral judgments, precepts, and principles using moral permissibility and moral impermissibility. Since whatever is morally obligatory is a subset of what is morally permissible, we can initially work with the two moral categories: the morally permissible and the morally impermissible. (I will occasionally use the letters "MP" to express the property *being morally permissible*, and "MI" to express the property *being morally impermissible*.)

Property Complementarity

Since it is obvious that nothing can be both MP and MI at the same time, it is clear that MP and MI are complements; that is, anything that has one of these properties cannot have the other also. A true moral theory must be logically consistent, and that means any moral theory must respect the complementarity of MP and MI.

For many moral theories this requirement can appear to be a problem. Normative moral theories frequently include moral precepts that seem to generate inconsistency. Consider the tired example of a Nazi asking a woman who is hiding Jews in her house whether she is hiding any Jews. Some moral theories assert the moral precept *not telling the truth is morally impermissible*, so following the precept requires that one should tell the Nazi about the hidden Jews. But if the same moral theory holds the moral precept *putting anyone's life in severe danger is morally impermissible* following the precept requires that one not tell the Nazi about the hidden Jews. So on this moral theory telling the Nazi about the hidden Jews is both morally permissible and morally impermissible. Some moral theories do not provide a means for sorting out this kind of problem, even though there are a number of ways to do so. (For example, a theory could present a reasonable procedure for prioritizing its precepts.) For our present purposes, the point is that MP and MI are complements, such that any property that

---

it is important to distinguish what is necessary and what is merely possible. Metaphysicians have the advantage of a vocabulary that includes "necessary" and "contingent," and p is contingent entails p is not necessary. Thus there is available a way of speaking of which makes the same distinction without violating ordinary English use. Sadly, there is no term that *functions like* "contingent" for "morally permissible."

Basic Moral Propositions

is MI cannot also be MP, and any property that is MP cannot also be MI. From this it follows that *telling a Nazi the truth about hidden Jews* is either MI or MP, but not both. The complementarity of MP and MI serves a very important purpose in the logic of a moral theory, for with it a moralist can determine what moral property something has by knowing that it lacks its complement: what lacks MP is MI, and what lacks MI is MP.

How one derives MP from MI or MI from MP depends on the kind of complements the properties are. There are two different kinds of complements, absolute and relative. Absolute complements are such that *anything* which lacks one property has the other property, and nothing has both.[4] For example, *being a tree* and *not being a tree* are properties that are absolute complements—everything has one or the other. Since the number one lacks *being a tree*, it has *not being a tree*, that is, the number one is not a tree. My puppy lacks *being a tree*; she has the property of *not being a tree*.[5] So the question is, are MP and MI absolute complements? Is it true that anything that is not morally permissible is morally impermissible and vice versa? There is a decisive reason for thinking that they are not. Some things are neither MP nor MI; for examples, a computer or a rabbit. If someone asserted, say, that *this rabbit is morally permissible*, the fitting response would be to say the speaker had made a category mistake—that rabbits are not the kind of things that are either MP or MI. And the same is true of a computer. MP and MI are not properties of objects, they are most

---

4. More formally stated,

(1) Properties F and G are absolute complements, if and only if for all x, x is F if and only if x lacks G. [from which it follows that for all x, x is G if and only if x lacks F.]

When the expression "if and only if" connects two propositions, it means that the two propositions have the same truth value. (For brevity it is often written simply as "iff.") If one proposition is true, the other one is also; if one proposition is false, the other one is also. This relationship is called "logical equivalence" and is symbolized with a double arrow ($\leftrightarrow$). The symbol (x) simply means "for all x." When one proposition (say, Lx) entails another (say, Tx) it means that if Lx is true, then Tx is true. Entailment is symbolized with an arrow, thus (x)(Lx $\rightarrow$ Tx). Finally, when x lacks property G, it is written with a squiggly horizontal line before the property, thus '~Gx' means 'x lacks G.' So (1) stated symbolically is (1) (Properties F and G are absolute complements) $\leftrightarrow$(x)[(Fx $\leftrightarrow$ ~ Gx) and (x)(Gx $\leftrightarrow$ ~Fx)], which would be read "Properties F and G are absolute complements, if and only for anything x, it is F if and only if it is not-G, and it is G if and only if it is not-F." In fact, both of these conjuncts are not necessary since (x)(Fx $\leftrightarrow$ ~Gx) is logically equivalent to (x)(~Fx $\leftrightarrow$ Gx). So (1) can be written, (1) (Properties F and G are absolute complements) iff (x)(Fx $\leftrightarrow$ ~Gx).

5. Properties where one is simply lacking the other, as in the example, are the clearest cases of absolute complements.

obviously properties of individual acts.[6] Asserting *this computer is morally impermissible* involves a category mistake by attributing a specific property to something that does not take properties of that kind. Attributing properties outside their possible extension is what metaphors do.[7] Literally speaking, some things are neither MP nor MI; they are outside the extension of these moral properties.[8]

If MP and MI are not absolute complements, then they must be *relative complements*. Two properties are relative complements if they are complements with respect to some set(s) of things, but not complements with respect to everything.[9] For example, *being even* or *being odd* are relative complements with respect to integers between 1 and 50. Every number in that group is either even or odd, but not both. For two properties to be relative complements requires some set or category within which the properties are complementary. *Passing the course* and *failing the course* are complementary properties for persons taking and finishing the course for credit.[10] They are not properties of the professor of the course, the president of the school, or anyone not enrolled for credit.

Notice that the categories within which two properties are relative complements can be of varying size. *Being even* and *being odd* are relative complements with respect to integers between one and fifty, but they are also relative complements with respect to integers between one and ten million, and an infinite number of other sets. Of interest for moral theorizing is

---

6. Exactly what kind of acts, and the moral properties of objects, will be taken up in chapter 5.

7. The "extension" of a property is those things which have it. The "possible extension" of a property is those things that could have it.

8. So $(x)(MPx \leftrightarrow \sim MIx)$ is false. That is, some things are neither MP nor MI. Perhaps, however, they have other moral properties; for example, they may be morally good or morally bad. We shall see how this could be in chapter 4.

9. Of course, everything either has a property or lacks it, but note: lacking a property is not the same as having its complement when they are relative complements. When two properties are absolute complements anything lacking a property must have its complement.

10. Let's say that any such category is comprised of things that have the property C. Then we can say that (2) Properties A and B are relative complements with respect to a property C if and only if for anything x, if it is C then it is A if and only if it is ~B. For example, being even and being odd are relative complements with respect to numbers between 1 and 50 if and only if for all x, if x is a number between 1 and 50, then x is even if and only if x is not odd.

maximal relative complementarity, the complementarity with respect to *all* of the things for which two moral properties are complementary.

Maximal Relative Complements

This idea of maximal relative complementarity is not a difficult idea to grasp, but it is complicated to explain. I'll start by giving a formal definition and then explicate it as simply as I can. The definition of *maximal relative complements* is

> Properties A and B are maximal relative complements with respect to a property C if and only if for anything x, it is C if and only if it is A if and only if it lacks B.[11]

This definition says two things, first, that each thing in the category of things that are C is either A or B, but not both. (So far this is merely *relative complementarity*.) The second thing that the definition says is that there is nothing outside the category C that is either A or B. For example, consider again the case of integers. Let C be the category of integers, and let A be *even* and B be *odd*. Each integer is even or odd, and no integer is both. Additionally, nothing that is not an integer is even or odd. (I have a few relatives that are odd, but the property in view here is the arithmetic one.) The property of *being an integer* is a maximal property with respect to *being even* and *being odd* because everything that is an integer is either even or odd, and nothing that is not an integer can be either one. My computer falls outside the maximal property of things for which even and odd are complementary properties. (Of course, *being even* or *not being even* are absolute complements—everything is one or the other.)

---

11. Stated symbolically, (3) Properties A and B are maximal relative complements with respect to a property C iff (x)(Cx ↔ (Ax ↔ ~Bx)). Notice that the difference between two properties that are relative complements with respect to some property C, and two properties that are relative complements with respect to a maximal property C is that, regarding the latter, the complementariness does not extend to anything that is not C. The only change between (2) and (3) is that where (2) says x is C entails x is A iff x lacks B, (3) says x is C is logically equivalent to x is A iff x lacks B. So with integers, if one is not odd it must be even, and if it is not even it must be odd. But my computer is not an integer, so even though it cannot have the property of *being even*, it lacks the property *being odd*.

The Moral Field

Now how is this idea of maximal complementariness relevant to moral theories? We have already seen that MP and MI are not absolute complements, they are relative complements. Let's name the property with respect to which they are maximal relative complements "M." (So everything in M is either MP or MI, but not both; and nothing that is not M is either MP or MI.) Different moral theories identify M in different ways, yielding moral theories that cover various domains.[12] But they all implicitly or explicitly identify some property as the maximal property with respect to which MI and MP are relative complements. The category of things that are M for a moral theory S can be called "the *moral field* of S." So not only can moral theories differ as to which moral property something has, they can differ about what things can have moral properties.[13]

The payoff for recognizing the relationships between the properties MP, MI, and M is a logical economy. First, it ensures that a moral theory will be logically consistent by not allowing anything to be both MP and MI. Second, it makes clear that an often neglected feature of moral theorizing does matter, namely the extension of M, or the exact dimensions of the moral field. If we know the extension of any two of MI, MP, and M, then the extension of the third can be determined. So there is a logical economy gained by recognizing that MP and MI are maximal relative complements relative to M.

Now let's see how this works. A moral theory must explicitly or implicitly identify its moral field. Suppose a moral theory explains what it is for something to be MP. Then we know that anything in the moral field of the theory that lacks MP is MI. If it is something outside the moral field of the theory, then on the theory it is amoral—lacking any moral property. The difference between something x being MI and amoral depends on whether x is in the moral field (has M).[14] Typically a moral theorist attempts

---

12. More needs to be said about M and the idea of the extension of a property. Both of these are taken up in chapter 5 when the moral field of a theory is considered. As it stands, for each moral theory M could stand for different properties so long as they were all necessarily coextensive, that is, they necessarily range over the same things, which is to say, everything that has one property has the other.

13. The relationship of M, MP, and MI is that anything that is in the moral field (is M) must be either MP or MI (but not both), and anything that lacks M (and so is outside the moral field) is neither MP or MI. For anything, it is M if and only if—it is MP if and only if it lacks MI.

14. Sometimes the term "amoral" is used in the sense of being morally

to identify with some precision the extension of MP or MI and assumes, without much consideration, the extension of M. As has been shown, however, the identity of the moral extension is not a trivial feature of a moral theory. Either it, or both MI and MP, need to be explicated in a complete moral theory.

Moral Judgments

There are three kinds of moral propositions: particular moral judgments (or simply "moral judgments"), moral precepts, and moral principles. We will consider the first two of these in what follows, reserving moral principles for the next chapter.

Moral properties can be properly attributed to a variety of things. We may say, "Laura is a good person"; or we may say "impatience is morally wrong"; or we may say, "civil freedom is a good thing." Thus we attribute moral properties to people, traits, states of affairs, and also acts. For our present purposes, we will use *acts* as the things to which moral properties are attributed. People say things like, "leaving the restaurant without paying your bill was immoral," or "it was good that you told the truth to your mother yesterday." Restricting ourselves at present to acts, rather than states of affairs, traits or any other kind of member of the moral field, allows us to get a handle on a narrower range of moral property holders before considering the wider possibilities.

Act-Tokens

The distinction between particular moral judgments and moral precepts depends on the understanding *act-tokens* and *act-types*.[15] An act-token is a single, specific, non-repeatable act, like John Wilkes Booth's shooting of Abraham Lincoln. An act-token has a particular moral agent, and takes place at specific place and time. For the present, the assumption is that each act-token is in M, the moral field, and thus it is either morally permissible or morally impermissible.[16] Attributing a moral property to an act-token

---

impermissible—and beneath contempt on top of that. But moralists use it in its literal sense—lacking any moral property, that is, being outside the moral field.

15. This distinction was explained in brief in chapter 2.
16. In chapter 5 this assumption will be considered more carefully.

(or any other individual thing) results in a *particular moral judgment*, or more simply, a *moral judgment*.

Most act-tokens are morally uninteresting: Alvin's choosing to wear his brown loafers on May 10, 2012 at 7:34 a.m. is morally permissible, and of little moral interest. The same is true of most of the act-tokens moral agents do. Each day almost every person performs hundreds of moral act-tokens, most of them trivial, such as which fruit to have for lunch or which shoe to put on first. Some have thought that such trivial acts have no moral properties, that they are amoral—outside of M. On our present assumption, however, each act-token has a moral property. Most trivial act-tokens are morally permissible, and are not very morally interesting. Some act-tokens, however, are neither trivial nor morally uninteresting.

Identifying and Expressing Act-Tokens

A major problem in forming particular moral judgments is individuating, identifying and describing the act-token to which a moral property is being attributed in a moral judgment. It is particularly difficult to individuate act-tokens. Consider Tom who goes out into the forest, hangs a target on a tree, aims his pistol at the target, pulls the trigger, shoots his pistol, misses his target, and shoots a forest ranger who subsequently dies of his wound. How many acts occurred? Just one? Many? Tom moved his finger pulling the trigger. Tom aimed his pistol. Tom shot the pistol. Tom missed the target. Tom shot a forest ranger. Tom accidentally shot a forest ranger. Tom killed a forest ranger. If these are all distinct act-tokens, then they each have moral properties. Some of the act-tokens that Tom did are MP (morally permissible), such as moving his finger to pull the trigger; some of them are MI, like killing a forest ranger. But is it true that Tom did multiple acts? The earlier example of an act-token was John Wilkes Booth's shooting of Abraham Lincoln. Clearly this act included a whole complex including Booth's intentions, his choices, his physical movements, and consequences of what he did. Are each of these are distinct act-tokens? Is Booth's decision to shoot Lincoln a distinct act-token? Is his aiming the pistol at Lincoln's head a distinct act-token? Is his pulling the trigger a distinct act-token? Is Lincoln's being killed a distinct act-token? And most important, do each of these have its own moral property?

It is customary to think of every distinct act-token as having its own moral property. What is critical to note, however, is that some act-tokens

Basic Moral Propositions

are composites of other act-tokens. The act-token of John Wilkes Booth's shooting of Abraham Lincoln is a composite of a large set of act-tokens. Consider each of these individual act tokens. Does each of these distinct act-tokens have its own moral property? Is Booth's decision to shoot Lincoln a distinct act-token with its own moral property? Is his aiming the pistol at Lincoln's head a distinct act-token with its own moral property? Is his pulling the trigger a distinct act-token with its own moral property? Is Lincoln's being killed a distinct act-token with its own moral property?

Consider the case of Tom again. One of the act-tokens that he did was aiming the pistol. Clearly this act-token is not the whole story; it is just part of what Tom did. In making moral judgments we are not typically interested in the moral properties of each of the constituent act-tokens of some human doing. Rather, we are interested in the morality of a more complete act-token. We can, if we choose, focus on constituent act-tokens and ask about the morality of them. So we could ask whether Tom's aiming the pistol is MP or MI. But typically we are interested in the whole chain of intentions, choices, movements, and consequences that together compose what I will call an *event act-token*.

An event act-token is a set of act-tokens done by the same moral agent(s) that cluster together in time and can be thought of a composite act-token, a single doing. An event act-token comprises the decisions, the plans, the intentions that lead to a doing, and some of the act-tokens may be the causal consequences of what is done. These predecessors and consequences cluster around some central doing that often gives the entire event act-token its identity. The central doing of Tom was firing his pistol at a target and accidentally killing a forest ranger. The proximate act-tokens that led to this central doing and the proximate consequences that followed from it are part of the cluster that comprise what Tom did.

Particular moral judgments should refer to an act-token in a way that identifies it as a unique act-token. In most contexts this is not difficult, as the one making the judgment and those who hear or read it understand which act is being referred to. The one making the judgment refers to it briefly, in a kind of shorthand. "What Tom did was simply wrong!" someone asserts, and all who know what happened know what he's talking about. Still, such act-token referrals can easily be mistaken. Frequently, the way of referring to the act under consideration determines its moral status. "Tom murdered a person" entails that Tom did something morally impermissible. If you listen to people arguing, you regularly hear them describe what happened in ways that favor their position. "You lied to me" is one description; "I protected you from having your feelings hurt" is quite another.

Most particular moral judgments attribute a moral property to an event act-token. The terms used in the judgment are often unclear as to exactly which event act-token is being referenced. For example, a person could say, "What Tom did yesterday was morally impermissible." The subject of this attribution is not clear, as Tom did many things yesterday. What the judgment maker is assuming is that the hearer understands the referent, and so knows what she is talking about. A problem can arise when the words used to refer to the event act-token are misunderstood or misleading. If one simply said, "Tom's shooting his pistol yesterday was morally wrong," it would be hard to know with enough precision what event act-token was being referred to. Does it include his hitting the forest ranger and killing him? Does it include that Tom was aiming at a target but missed badly?

The term "event act-token" refers to single act-tokens and consequences that are proximately connected to one another in time and space. This term can be used to refer to something very limited in time or be stretched to include months or years. So both "Chad's decision to cheat . . ." and "The U.S.A. entering World War II . . ." are event act-tokens, the former possibly comprised of just one act-token, the latter involving hundreds of act-tokens. Event act-tokens can themselves be parts of still larger event act-tokens, like "Taking a history course . . ." is part of "Taking courses to get a college degree . . ." The assertion "World War II was an immoral war" is a particular moral judgment since World War II is an event act-token. But it is not a very specific one. The clearest particular moral judgments are quite specific about the event act-token that is involved. To know what event act-token is being referred to generally requires one specify its agent(s) and time frame. It is important in any particular moral judgment that the referent used to single out the event act-token is made clear. In some contexts this may require some significant description, to include all the circumstances, agents, and deeds done. In other contexts it may suffice to simply say, "What Tom did yesterday . . ." in a context where everyone knows what Tom did yesterday. Identifying the moral property of an event act-token usually requires information of the act's historical and social context, the act's effects, and

Basic Moral Propositions

the agent's intentions and beliefs. In conversation or in writing it is not always convenient to include all of this in the words that are used to refer to the event act-token, so often a kind of shorthand description is used to refer to the whole complex of features relevant to a moral understanding of the act. A moral judgment is well formed only when the words used to refer to the event act-token are understood well enough so that one can identify, more or less, the cluster of act-tokens that comprise the event act-token that is the subject of the judgment. The category of act-tokens includes both individual act-tokens and event act-tokens.

This ontology of act-tokens leads us to consider what the relationship is between the moral properties of the constituent act-tokens to the event act-token of which they are a part. Initially, one natural supposition is to think that the relationship is such that if one act-token that is part of an event act-token is impermissible, then the event act-token is impermissible. But this is not always the case. Consider a person's donating three million dollars to a worthwhile charity for hidden, selfish reasons. The act-token of being motivated by selfishness may be MI, but the event act-token is MP. So an event act-token could be MP even if some of the act-tokens in it are MI. Another possibility is that any event act-token that is MI must have at least one act-token that is part of it which is MI; no set of act-tokens that together comprise a morally impermissible event act-token can each be MP—if an event act-token is MI, then at least one of the act-tokens that are part of it must be MI. This seems right. Many event act-tokens that are MI are comprised of many moral tokens that are MP, but there must always be at least one act-token that is MI. It would also seem that if an event act-token is morally obligatory, then at least some of its act-tokens are morally obligatory.[17]

Particular moral judgments can be true or false whether the act-token is actual or not. If one describes a hypothetical act-token and attributes a moral property to it, then what is asserted is *if the identified act-token were actual, then it would have the moral property*. The conditions under which such assertions are true are similar to that of hypothetical (and even counterfactual claims.[18] So, for example, two people could argue about whether Hamlet's decision to kill the king was morally permissible or not. Or sup-

---

17. I leave it to the reader to consider whether there are any other logical relationships between the morality of the act tokens that are components of an event act-token and the morality of the event act-token itself.

18. The issue of counter-factuals will come up again in the next chapter when the modality of moral propositions is considered.

pose Jeremy contemplated telling the police where to find Sam, his friend and drug dealer, but decided not to do so. One might say, contrary to fact, that if Jeremy had told the police about Sam, it would have been morally permissible. People frequently make hypothetical claims, and even argue about them, and people often make moral claims about fictional event act-tokens. So there are often claims about the moral lapses of Hamlet or King Lear. This is not a problem; it merely needs to be understood that these are attributions of moral properties to fictional (event) act-tokens, and understood to mean that if the hypothetical event act-token were actual, it would have the moral property attributed. They are *hypothetical particular moral judgments*.

Moral Precepts

We each have some acquaintance with moral precepts, and they seem straightforward enough. Someone says, "Stealing is morally wrong" and everyone assumes we know what is meant and we agree. But moral precepts and the conditions under which they are true or false are rather complicated.

The subject of moral precepts is not act-tokens but act-types. "Stealing" and "telling a lie" are examples of act-types. Act-types are *kinds* or *categories* of act-tokens. An act-token that is an instance of stealing is said to "fall under" the act-type of stealing. Obviously, each event act-token will fall under numerous act-types. So if Sarah tells a lie about Thad and thereby harms his reputation, we could say the event act-token falls under both the act-type telling a lie and stealing (Thad's good name). It also would fall under other act-types, like speaking to someone, speaking in English, and intending to deceive someone. An act-type is just that, a type or kind of act; examples include act-tokens done on Tuesdays, act-tokens done in the city limits of Cleveland, and act-tokens that are murders.

Most act-types are themselves morally uninteresting, particularly because the act-tokens that fall under the category they identify have different moral properties. So any attempt to use them in making a moral precept would result in a false assertion. Thus, *acts done on Tuesdays are MP (morally permissible)* is a moral precept, but obviously, since some of the acts done on Tuesdays are MI (morally impermissible), this moral precept is false. The same is true of act-tokens done in the city limits of Cleveland; they are not all MI or all MP.

Basic Moral Propositions

Both actual and hypothetical act-tokens can fall under an act-type. This complicates a bit the conditions under which a moral precept is true or false.[19] *Telling a lie is morally impermissible* will be true if all the actual act-tokens that fall under it are morally impermissible, and if all the possible act-tokens that would fall under it, if they were actual, would also be morally impermissible. The claim is that any act-token, actual or hypothetical, that falls under the kind or category "telling a lie" has or would be MI. In order to be true, a moral precept needs to be such that each act-token that falls under the act-type it employs, if it were it actual, would have the moral property the moral precept attributes.

Some act-types cover act-tokens of which the vast majority are MI, such as the act-token *punching someone*. Some act-types identify acts some of which are MP, and others that are not, like *something done by an English prime minister*. Some act-types identify acts that are almost always MP, like *offering to help someone*. The act-types that pick out act-tokens almost all of which share the same moral property are the most common and the most helpful. For example, almost every act-token that falls under the act-type telling a lie is MI, so *telling a lie is MI* is a helpful moral precept. Strictly speaking, however, it is false. Some act-tokens that involve telling a lie are MP. For example, it is morally permissible to lie to a home intruder about where a hidden child is. So the precept *telling a lie is morally impermissible* claims too much and needs to be qualified. Many of these common moral precepts are false because any act-token that falls under the act-type but that does not have the moral property the moral precept attributes will make the moral precept false. One needs to carefully articulate a moral precept so that the act-tokens that fall under it have or would have the same moral property. Even one possible act-token that falls under the act-type employed by the moral precept but lacks the moral property attributed by the precept is enough to make a moral precept false.

Certain act-types by definition entail that the act-tokens that fall under them have a particular moral property. For example, act-tokens that fall under *being a murder* are MI, since part of the meaning of "murder" is that it is morally impermissible. Precepts that use act-types that include the moral property in their definition cannot have exceptions—so *murder is MI* is necessarily true. One problem is that this is of little help in trying to determine if a specific killing is morally wrong. Suppose some Nazi

---

19. As we have seen in chapter 2, the truth conditions for a moral precept depend on the truth value of the particular moral judgments that fall under it.

general had succeeded in assassinating Hitler. Would that have been morally wrong? What if the general killed Hitler in 1932, before Hitler came to power? Would that have been murder? Moral precepts that are necessarily true (by definition) are not usually very helpful. The issue simply shifts to whether the act-token falls under the act-type.

In *The Theory of Morality* Alan Donagan formulates his moral precepts frequently using the phrase "at will" to qualify act-tokens. So he says, for example, "It is impermissible for any human being to take his own life at will." This allows him to say that some suicides are not impermissible. What does he mean by adding "at will?" One interpretation leads to the conclusion that he means that phrase to exclude all the exceptions to the rule.[20] So suicide is morally impermissible if done at will means that it is MI except when it is not. And while this makes the precepts using "at will" true, it also makes them not very helpful. A second interpretation takes Donagan to use "at will" to mean "on purpose." There are two different ways an agent can do an act-token on purpose. One is simply that the agent intends to do the act-token that he or she does and therefore the agent is responsible for the act. The suicide of a madman is not the act of a moral agent. A better way to read "at will" as "on purpose" takes it for something like "chosen for its own sake." On this reading Donagan intends to eliminate those act-tokens where the agent has other ends in view which justify or condemn the act-token. For example, he has in mind suicides undertaken for great or noble causes, like hanging oneself in a cell rather than betraying significant military secrets under torture. In Donagan's language, such acts are not suicide *at will*, that is, not done for its own sake, and so it does not fall under the act-type "suicide at will." Thus understood, for Donagan suicide as an end in itself is always morally impermissible, but as a means to some other ends it may be permissible.[21]

The problem with this way of expressing moral precepts is that very often agents undertake acts as a means to some other end or ends. When a person punches another, for example, it is not generally done for its own sake, the thrill of striking the blow, but for some other reason, such as to protect the puncher or punish the punched. In many cases the precept *for anybody to use force upon another at will is MI* will not cover punching.

---

20. Donagan, *Theory of Morality*, 73.

21. Interpreted this way virtually all of Donagan's first order precepts require this sort of narrowing of the act-token to deeds done for their own sakes, thus excluding them from falling under the act-type deeds done for the sake of some other end.

Basic Moral Propositions

A helpful moral precept, like a helpful proverb, is an accurate summary of the morality of a commonly used act-type, act-types like *lying to someone* or *stealing from someone*. Such useful precepts are sometimes said to be true, and they may be when the act-type in the precept is understood. The moral precept *telling lies is morally MI* must be understood not as *all instances of telling a lie are MI*, but rather as *telling a lie is almost always MI*. Thus exegeted, moral precepts are helpful guides to moral discernment. Strictly speaking, however, many of the commonly used moral precepts are false. They fall short of the kind of rigor that avoids any possible counter examples. For a moral precept to be true requires the identification of the act-type that limits the actual and possible act-tokens falling under it to those sharing the same moral property. Additionally, as we have seen, for a moral precept to be helpful, the act-type should not entail the moral property attributed. Thus, while moral precepts are useful in ordinary contexts as a kind of shorthand for making and assessing particular moral judgments, it turns out that moral precepts are of limited value in articulating a philosophical moral theory.

Moral Rules

Finally, the idea of a morally permissible rule[22] is useful even though such rules are not moral propositions and are not part of the moral order. A morally permissible rule is a norm that does not attribute a moral property to anything, but rather prescribes some specific human conduct. Thus mothers make rules for their children, like *you may not ride your bike in the street*. Governments make lots of rules or laws that prescribe conduct, like *pay an amount equal to 6% of every purchase to the government as a tax*. Some of these rules may prescribe doing act-tokens that are morally impermissible. Such a rule would be an immoral rule. In contrast, a morally permissible rule is *any rule that does not require any agent to ever do any act-token that is morally impermissible*.

This is not to say that following a morally permissible rule will always result in morally permissible acts. One can follow the morally permissible rule to drive on the right side of the road and still intentionally

---

22. Although it is verbally cumbersome, I will use the longer name "morally permissible rule." A "moral rule" is ambiguous: it can be a rule that is moral as opposed to immoral; moral as opposed to amoral; or morally obligatory as opposed to morally permissible.

57

hit a pedestrian and flee the scene. An immoral rule can be defined as *an immoral rule is any rule that requires an act-token that is morally impermissible*. The idea of a moral rule is helpful in evaluating the positive laws and practical rules that are operative in a political community or culture.

Conclusion

In this chapter we have considered particular moral judgments, moral precepts, and moral rules. Moral judgments and moral precepts are two important kinds of moral propositions that attribute moral properties. Rightly used these could be conjoined to express a complete moral theory, but normally such theories are expressed in terms of a *moral principle*. In the next chapter we will consider the logical structure of moral principles.

4

Moral Principles

Each day we are confronted with multiple choices of what to do and what to say. Many of these choices are relatively trivial, and we easily fall into patterns of behavior. In such cases our choices are habitual. I almost always drive the same route to my work; maybe you always shop in the same grocery store, or eat lunch at the same café. Almost every day, however, most of us will face choices for which we have no routine. Perhaps you are going to vote and you aren't sure which candidates to vote for; or a friend asks you what you think about her idea to divorce her husband; or you are wondering if you should tell your parents about the traffic ticket you got. Situations like this challenge us, and we need to navigate the alternatives carefully. The limits of what we may say or do are set by the moral order, which lays out what is permitted, required, and forbidden. So we need some grasp of the moral order. To have a deeper understanding of the moral order requires having a moral theory.[1] A moral theory is a theory that lays out a way to identify and distinguish what is morally permissible (MP), what is morally obligatory (MO), and what is morally impermissible (MI).[2] A moral theory provides a basis for answering questions about what a person may do, must do, and should not do.

---

1. For a single decision you don't usually need a whole moral theory, although having one provides a means for justifying specific judgments.
2. Alternatively, moral theory can provide a way to distinguish what is morally good and morally bad. Because moral properties can be derived from one another, as I indicated in chapter 3 and will show in chapter 5, it does not matter very much which moral properties are used in expressing a moral theory.

Ethics deals with the moral order. There are many hundreds of books about moral theory, and most of them are hundreds of pages long, yet the surprising truth is that the essence of a moral theory can be expressed in a single sentence—a moral principle.[3] Books that lay out a particular moral theory often start first by identifying and explaining the moral principle of the theory, arguing for the moral principle against rival proposals and possible objections, and showing what results the identified moral principle produces in a variety of situations. Basically, a moral principle identifies everything that is moral (as opposed to amoral) into what is MP and what is MI (or what is MG and what is MB).

This is the most technically challenging chapter in the book. In this chapter I will explain three things. First, since a moral principle needs to achieve certain goals, it needs to meet some logical conditions. The simplest and clearest way to meet these conditions is to have a certain logical structure, which I explain. This is a very important issue and is rather technical, but I try to make it as clear as possible. Second, after recognizing that the logical structure of a moral principle involves a link between a moral property and a non-moral property, I circumscribe the exact nature of this link. Finally, I address the issue of the *modality* of moral principles; that is, are they necessary or merely contingent?[4]

In this chapter I assume some of the ideas that have been explained in the previous chapter on moral judgments. One important relationship that will be used is the idea of a maximal set with respect to which two properties are relative complements.[5] Recall that properties A and B are *relative complements* when every member in category C is either A or B but not both. *Maximal* relative complementarity adds to this that there is nothing outside of C that is either A or B. Maximal relative complementarity entails that if something is either A or B, it is in category C. For example, *being an integer* (category C) is the maximal property for the two relative complements *being odd* (A) and *being even* (B). Every integer is either odd or even, and nothing that is not an integer is either odd or even.

---

3. Although there are alternative ways of expressing a moral theory, as we shall see. But even most of those can be recast as a moral principle.

4. In chapter 7 I will explain what kinds of non-moral properties could be linked to moral properties. This turns out to be an interesting and controversial topic, giving rise to different varieties of moral theories, like natural law and divine command theory.

5. Two properties are relative complements if they are complements with respect to some sets of things, but not complements with respect to everything.

Moral Principles

The reason this relationship is important will become clearer in this chapter, but recall that the moral properties *being morally permissible* (MP) and *being morally impermissible* (MI) are relative complements. The maximal property with respect to which they are relative complements I gave the designation "M." Each member and only members of the set of things that are M are either MP or MI, but not both. Something cannot be both MP and MI, just as an integer cannot be both odd and even. Moreover, nothing that has either of the relative complements MP or MI will be outside of the category M, just as nothing could be either odd or even and be outside the category of *being an integer*.

Since M is the maximal property for the complements MP and MI, it identifies the category that includes everything that is moral (as opposed to amoral).[6] I will call this set of things *the moral field*. Since different moral theories may identify M differently, we can speak of those things that are M in a particular theory S as *the moral field of S*. In chapter 5 we will consider the moral field.

The Basic Logical Structure of Moral Principles

A moral theory needs to distinguish what is MI and what is MP. The way this is most clearly done is with a moral principle. A well-formed moral principle does two things: it identifies the moral field of the theory, identifying what kinds of things are in the moral field that are either MP or MI, and then gives a way to distinguish what is MP and what is MI in the moral field. A moral principle separates out in the moral field the sheep and the goats, what is MP and what is MI. Since whatever lacks MP in the moral field will be MI (and vice versa), a moral principle only needs to identify what is MP (or what is MI) and everything else in the field will be MI (or MP). To distinguish the sheep and goats one only needs to separate out the sheep—the rest are goats (or vice versa). So if a person only knows what a sheep is, he can still separate sheep and goats, if he knows that every animal in the pen is either a sheep or a goat. In a similar way, if a moralist can clearly identify what is MI in the moral field, then he is able to distinguish everything that is MI from what is MP in the moral field.

---

6. *Being moral* and *being amoral* are absolute complements (*everything* is either one or the other, but nothing is both).

Let us look at two examples of a moral principle drawn from philosophical tradition. Fred Feldman, in his handy little book *Introductory Ethics* expresses the moral principle of J. S. Mill as follows:

(1) An act is right if and only if there is no other act the agent could have done instead that has a higher utility than it has.[7]

(1) uses the term "right" meaning, of course, "morally right," and it is most reasonable to assume that Mill means it to refer to the property of *being morally obligatory*.[8] For Mill, an agent is morally obliged to choose the act available to her that maximizes utility. This moral principle assumes *acts* are included in M; thus acts are in the moral field. The way (1) is stated, however, does not allow us to say that acts compose the whole moral field. (1) only implies that acts are in the moral field. We sometimes speak of a person as morally good or morally bad, that is, as having a moral property, but Mill's principle, as understood by Feldman, is not about persons. (1) does not directly tell us any moral truth about persons.

(1) states that an act is MO if and only if it has a specific non-moral property, the property *being an act such that there is no other act the agent could do that would have higher utility*. Exactly what Mill means by "higher utility" is not important for our purposes; it is enough to say that it has to do with the consequences of the act. To see the logical structure of the moral principle more clearly (even without fully grasping Mill's idea) we can assign the letter "U" to this non-moral property *being an act such that there is no other act the agent could do that would have higher utility*. Then the structure of Feldman's version of Mill's principle is:

(1a) If x is an act, then x is MO if and only if x is U.[9]

In another chapter, Feldman states the categorical imperative of Kant as follows:

(2) An act is morally right if and only if the agent of the act can consistently will that the generalized form of the maxim of the act be a law of nature.[10]

---

7. Feldman, *Introductory Ethics*, 26. This formulation suffers from the ambiguity of "morally right" as will the example from Kant. It turns out, I think, that the moral property being referred to is different in the two cases.

8. Whether Feldman (or Mill) intended to identify acts that are MP or MO does not matter to my present use of the principle.

9. Stated symbolically, $(x)((Ax) \rightarrow (MPx \equiv Ux))$

10. Feldman, *Introductory Ethics*, 104.

Moral Principles

This formulation of the categorical imperative has the same logical structure as (1). The differences are that I think that the best way to understand "is morally right" in (2) is with the property *being morally permissible* (MP) rather than *being morally obligatory* (MO). And the non-moral property for Kant is also different from Mill's. For Kant the non-moral property is *being an act such that the agent of the act can consistently will that the generalized form of the maxim of the act be a law of nature*. Again, without having a perfectly clear idea what property Kant is referring to, we can designate this non-moral property "G." So the logical structure of Feldman's version of Kant's principle is:

(2a) If x is an act, then x is MP if and only if x is G.[11]

So we can see that (1a) and (2a) have the same logical structure (although they employ different moral properties and different non-moral properties). We may not know exactly what non-moral properties each is using, but it is clear that they are not using the same one.

To represent this logical structure, we need to use *property variables*. A property variable is a letter that can stand for one property out of a range of properties. For example, we could say that the letter D is a property variable that ranges over color properties. Then instances of D would be *is red* or *is blue* or some other color property. In order to clearly show the logical structure of a moral principle, we need some property variables. To express a moral principle we need one pair of property variables to represent any moral property and its relative complement. We will let "MM" be a property variable that ranges over moral properties, and "MC" stand for the relative complement of MM. There are only two possible pairs of properties that "MM" and "MC" can stand for—when "MM" stands for MP (*being morally permissible*), then "MC" stands for MI (*being morally impermissible*); and when "MM" stands for MG (*being morally good*), then "MC" stands for MB (*being morally bad*). We need a second property variable to range over all non-moral properties. In (1) and (2) above we used "G" and "U" to stand for the non-moral properties, but now we need a variable that will range over any non-moral property, and for that we will use "NM." (To help remember these property variables and their ranges, note that MM ranges over <u>m</u>oral properties, MC is the <u>m</u>oral <u>c</u>omplement of MM, and NM ranges over <u>n</u>on-<u>m</u>oral properties.) Now we can state the general form of a moral principle so far as follows:

---

11. Stated symbolically, $(x)((Ax) \rightarrow (MPx \circ Gx))$

(3) if x is an act, then (x is MM if and only if x is NM).[12]

Let's consider how this would go with a particular case. Suppose MM is the property MP, and NM is the property *causing the agent more pleasure than pain*. If the act in question is John's using heroin tonight, then (3) would entail

(4) If John uses heroin tonight, then this act is morally permissible (MP) if and only if it causes John more pleasure than pain.

So a moral principle says whether something in the moral field has a specific moral property, in this instance MP, based on whether it has some specific non-moral property.

So far, so good. We can more clearly display this structure if we learn two logical symbols for the relationships connecting the proposition *x is an act*, the proposition *x is MM*, and the proposition *x is NM*. One way logicians display *if p then q* is to use an arrow: $p \rightarrow q$. This means "if p, then q" or "p entails q." The proposition *p if and only if q* means that both $p \rightarrow q$ and $q \rightarrow p$, and one way logicians display that relationship is with a double arrow: $p \leftrightarrow q$. The double arrow symbol is called a "bi-conditional."

With these symbols, we see that the most general logical structure of (3) is $p \rightarrow q$, with the antecedent p (*x is an act*) and the consequent q (*x is MM $\leftrightarrow$ x is NM*). The consequent displays that a moral principle links a moral property with a non-moral one, a linkage that we will consider in the next section. Before considering this linkage, however, we need to take a closer look at the general link between antecedent p (*x is an act*) and the consequent q *(x is MM $\leftrightarrow$ x is NM)*.

The Moral Field in a Moral Principle

As currently expressed in (3) what seems to comprise the moral field of the theory are *acts*. But even this is not clear, because the primary logical connector in (3) simply says that if something is an act, then the consequent is true. It does not say anything about things that are not acts, leaving open the possibility that the consequent may be true for something other than an act. If I say *if x is a apple, then x is a fruit*, I have said something true, but I haven't said anything about oranges which are also fruits. As stated (3) says something about acts, but it does not limit moral properties to acts. Thus, (3) does not identify the moral field of a moral theory, something that a moral principle needs to do.

12. Stated symbolically, $(x)((Mx \rightarrow (MMx \leftrightarrow NMx))$

Moral Principles

A purported moral principle that does not identify the whole moral field and covers only a part of the moral field is more like a moral precept. As we have seen in chapter 3, moral precepts only cover that part of the moral field identified by some act-type. The problem is that when a purported moral principle covers only some of the moral field, there are things that have moral properties which it does not address. For example, what does (3) tell us about Charles, whom everyone says is a morally good man. Is it the case that for Charles the consequent of (3) is true? According to (3), we can't tell, because Charles is not an act. If we amend the antecedent of (3) so that it covers the whole moral field of a moral theory, then as a result of how we amend it either Charles is in the moral field and the consequent tells us what moral property he has, or Charles is not in the moral field, so he cannot be morally good inasmuch as he does not have any moral property.

A moral principle needs to identify the moral field of the theory.[13] Feldman's formulation of the moral principles of Mill and Kant fails to delineate the moral field clearly. Feldman's version of a moral principle would be more accurate if it made clear that if—and only if—something is an act, then the consequent is true. This shows that what is needed is not a simple arrow between the antecedent and consequent in (3), but rather a double arrow. In a moral principle it is not just that if something is an act that the consequent follows, rather, it says that whenever the consequent is true, the antecedent is also true. So a moral principle is a compound proposition stating both

if x is an act then x is MM if and only if x is NM

and

if x is MM if and only if x is NM, then x is an act

In the present example we are taking it that acts comprise the moral field. In order to show that the moral principle covers the whole moral field, we need a double arrow between the antecedent and the consequent of (3). This shows that the principle covers the whole moral field of the theory.

(5) x is an act $\leftrightarrow$ (x is MM $\leftrightarrow$ x is NM).

(5) makes clear that each act and only acts have a moral property, and if an act has the non-moral property NM, then it has the moral property MM. (However, if an act lacks NM, then it has MC.) We can generalize this by

---

13. That is, of course, the maximal set of things that with respect to which MM and MC are relative complements.

using the symbol "M" for the moral field of a theory, and then we can substitute it in (5) so that it displays the logical structure of a moral principle more accurately.

(6) x is M ↔ (x is MM ↔ x is NM).[14]

The shorter way of stating "x is M" is simply "Mx," thus (6) becomes

(7) Mx ↔ (MMx ↔ NMx).

This formulation is shorter and general enough for all moral principles, regardless of what specific moral field, moral property, and non-moral property is used. What it says is that whatever is in the moral field (M) is such that it has a moral property MM if and only if it has a non-moral property NM, and anything that is both MM and NM is in the moral field. So using the same example as earlier, if "M" is *being an act* and MM is the property MP, and NM is the property *causing the agent more pleasure than pain* we get the following moral principle:

(8) x is an act if and only if (x is morally permissible if and only if x causes the agent more pleasure than pain).

From (7) it follows that everything that is M and lacks NM will have the moral property that is the relative complement of MM, that is MC. (The negation sign "~" in front of a property name indicates that something lacks the named property.) So (7) entails

(9) Mx ↔ (MCx ↔ ~NMx).

(9) says that anything in the moral field that lacks NM is MC, and anything that lacks NM and is MC is in the moral field. Using the example again, and remembering that the relative complement of MP is MI, this produces the moral principle:

(10) x is an act if and only if (x is MI if and only if x lacks the property of *causing the agent more pleasure than pain*).

So if any act has the property *causing the agent more pleasure than pain*, then it is morally permissible, but if it lacks that property, then the act is morally impermissible.

The logical connection of (7) and (9) makes it clear that a moral principle is a compound proposition.[15] The two propositions are, first, a claim

---

14. Recall that the symbol ↔ means "if and only if." (6) entails that for anything that is M (in the moral field), that if it is MM, then it is NM (it has some identified non-moral property); and vice versa—if it is NM, then it is MM.

15. Of course, not only does (7) entail (9), but (9) entails (7).

Moral Principles

about all the things that can have moral properties (the moral field), and, second, another compound proposition that links a non-moral property to a specific moral property for members of the moral field.

Now let's make this theoretical arrangement more concrete by considering an actual moral principle. One possible moral principle is

(11) x is an act ↔ (MPx ↔ God allows x)

This says is that for any act, and only for acts, if God allows it, it is morally permissible; and conversely, if it is morally permissible, then God allows it. The property *allowed by God* is not a moral property, so it is an instance of NM; the moral property in this principle is the moral property *is morally permissible*. So pick any act you want, it is in the moral field of this theory and it is either MP or MI. If it is an act that God allows, then it is MP; if not, it is MI; and nothing that is not an act is either MP or MI.

Now let's try to make the logic of moral principles as clear as possible. In plain English, the left side of the bi-conditional in (7) identifies everything in the moral field—everything that has either one moral property or its complement. We can picture this with an oval which is the moral field. Everything and only things inside the oval have a moral property; anything outside the circle is amoral, that is, lacking any moral property.

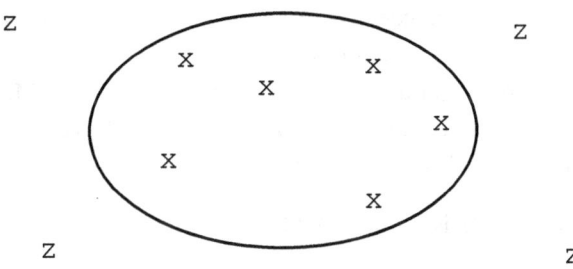

The consequent of a moral principle distinguishes which things in the moral field have one moral property (MM) rather than its moral property complement (MC). The way it makes this distinction is by linking one of the moral properties with some non-moral property (NM). Some things in the moral field are both MM and NM, and some things lack both. According to the principle, though, anything that lacks NM also lacks MM, so it has the complement MC. In making this distinction the moral theorist, as it were, draws a line clear across the moral field. Everything in the moral

67

field that is both NM and MM is on one side of the line, and everything on the other side of the line lacks NM and is MC.

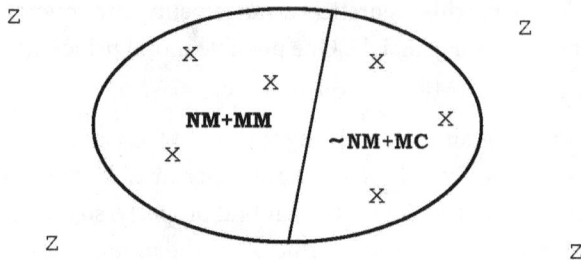

Two Observations about the Logical Structure of Moral Principles

Given the simplicity of this figure, it seems that there are ways other than by a moral principle by which one could distinguish MM and MC. For example, one could have a set of moral precepts which identify everything in the moral field as either MM or MC. Let's say that everything in the moral field can be sorted into three act-types, Q, R, and S. Precept 1 could tell us that "All Q are MM"; precept 2 is "All R are MC"; and precept 3 is "All S are MM." Now assuming the moral field is *acts*, this view could be expressed more simply: any act and only acts that are Q or S are MM. (So any act that is R has the complement of MM, that is, MC.) If we introduce a new property, T, which is "Q or S," we get

$$x \text{ is an act} \leftrightarrow (x \text{ is T} \leftrightarrow x \text{ is MM})$$

which has the structure of a moral principle symbolized in (6). So while listing precepts may seem a way of expressing a moral theory without using a moral principle, it will always be possible to conjoin or disjoin precepts in such a way as to create a moral principle. A moral principle may employ a complex non-moral property—like a disjunctive property or some conjunctive property—to express a moral principle, and the properties disjoined or conjoined need not be the same kinds of properties. In chapter 7, which discusses moral grounding, the whole issue of the kinds of non-moral properties identified in moral principles will be considered.

Moral Principles

Another important thing to note about moral principles is that two different ones could distinguish MM and MC in exactly the same way. If that occurred, we would say that the two principles are *logically equivalent*. For example, in Christian thought some have held that

x is an act ↔ (x is loving God ↔ x is morally permissible)

and

x is an act ↔ (x is loving your neighbor ↔ x is morally permissible)

distinguish what is MM from what is MC in the moral field exactly the same way. Thus there is no act that has the property of loving God that does not have the property of loving your neighbor, and vice versa. If this is true, then these two moral principles divide the moral field exactly the same way. It is worth noting that virtually all moral principles (proposed by serious moralists) are very similar in the way in which they distinguish MM and MC. No moral theorist comes to the view that it is morally permissible to torture small children, or to betray friends, or to break promises for no reason. A great deal of the moral field is pretty clearly MM or MC. The differences between moral principles is made apparent in difficult and controversial cases.

Historically, moral theorists have not dealt with identifying the moral field, although it is a topic I consider in chapter 5. They have focused most of their attention on identifying and explaining which non-moral property is linked to a moral property. Identifying this non-moral property is the most important way in which moral theories differ from each other. Suggestions as to the identity of a non-moral property that always occurs in conjunction with some moral property have been made throughout all of Western history, and have ranged from the natural to the spiritual.

Two questions regarding the general form of moral principles, i.e. (7) Mx ↔ (MMx ↔ NMx), need further consideration. First, more exactly, what is the nature of the link between MM and NM in a moral principle? Second, what is the modality of a moral principle, that is, is it necessary or contingent?

The Crucial Link in Moral Principles

Now we turn our attention to the right side of the double arrow in (/), that is, *x is MM if and only if x is NM* (otherwise expressed MMx ↔ NMx). This proposition links a non-moral property to a moral property: As stated, the consequent of a moral principle states a *logical equivalence*[16] between two propositions, one of which attributes a moral property to acts and one which attributes some non-moral property to acts. For example, the moral principle

(12) x is M ↔ (x is morally impermissible ↔ God forbids x).

The consequent of (12) links two propositions, *x is morally impermissible* and *God forbids x*. (12) says that everything M which is morally impermissible is forbidden by God *and* everything M forbidden by God is morally impermissible.

But we need to take a closer look at the relationship between the two propositions in the consequent of (12). Is logical equivalence the intended connection? Some moralists have proposed that the relationship between the non-moral property (NM) and moral property (MM) is weaker than logical equivalence. The idea is that NM (perhaps a conjunctive or disjunctive property) "supervenes" on MM, that is, something that is NM is, by that evidence, probably MM, but *x being NM* does not entail *x is MM*. John E. Hare explains how his father, R. M. Hare, makes use of the term "supervenience" by saying: "Value properties supervene on non-value properties, and that means that things have the value properties because they have the non-value properties. For example, a strawberry is good because it is sweet. But the value property is not the same as the non-value property, and ascribing the second does not entail ascribing the first."[17]

There are two things worth noting here. First, supervenience involves a kind of causality, so that the non-value properties bring it about, or cause, the value property. We will pick up this idea of causality below. The second thing to note is that supervenience is a relatively weak relationship. Consider the claim that an act's being reasonable and helpful supervenes on its being a morally permissible act. This claim of supervenience may be true, even when an act is reasonable and helpful and not morally permissible, as when a man gives an expensive watch that was obtained by fraudulent means to his wife. So an act's being reasonable and helpful may be evidence that it is morally permissible, but it does not entail it. The problem for our purposes with supervenience is that it is too weak to serve as the connection between NM and MM in a moral principle. Something could be NM and fail to be MM. Thus supervenience cannot carry much weight in an

---

16. A logical equivalence means that two propositions always have the same truth value, so if one is true, the other one is also.

17. Hare, *God's Call*, 9.

argument for what is MM. The existence of properties that supervene on a moral property—and there probably are such properties—is too weak and is inadequate for framing a moral theory.

Rather than logical equivalence being too strong to describe the relationship between the propositions in the consequent of (7), the fact is that it is too weak. For instance, a person who asserts (12) means to say more than that the two propositions *an act x is impermissible* and *God forbids x* are logically equivalent. (12) states that these two propositions are necessarily linked, yet (12) does not say enough about their connection. Consider what it does not say: it does not say that God's forbidding x is what *makes* x wrong; it does not say that that God's forbidding x *brings it about* that x is wrong; it does not say that God's forbidding x is *the reason why* x is morally wrong; it does not say that God forbids x *because* x is morally impermissible or that its moral impermissibility is *why* God forbids x. (12) merely states that the non-moral property *being forbidden by God* and the moral property of *being morally impermissible* are necessarily co-extensive: if something M has one, it has the other. Moral principles in the form of (6) do not give any explanation of why something has a specific moral property. They simply assert a logical equivalence, which is the strongest relationship possible in truth-functional logic, but fail to provide any explanation of the relationship between the states of affairs referred to by the propositions. From (12) we cannot tell whether an act is MI because God forbids it or if God forbids it because it is MI.[18] We don't want to dismiss logical equivalence as a vital part of the relationship, for with it we have a link between what is NM and what is MM.[19] Moral principles in the form of (7) can generate a moral theory. They can make it possible to distinguish those things that are M into those that are MM and those that are MC (the relative complement of MM for anything M). I will call those moral principles that do no more than attempt to make this distinction *moral system principles*. They can serve a vital purpose in helping to identify what is MM and MC, but they do not serve any explanatory function.[20]

Typically, moralists intend to assert more than that there is a logical link between some moral property and some non-moral property. They tell

18. Plato's *Euthyphro* shows the difference between these two, and I will say more about it in chapter 7.

19. They are not always so helpful in this identification, however, because sometimes the presence of NM is even more difficult to ascertain than that of MM.

20. Although some suggestions regarding NM are not much help, as when it is harder to figure out what is NM than what is MM.

us not only how to distinguish what is MM from MC, they explain to us what it is about something that makes it MM. If the moral field comprises acts, moralists want to explain *why* an act is morally permissible or impermissible. As it stands, (12) links what is impermissible and God's prohibition, but it does not provide any explanation for why such acts are morally wrong. My claim is that moral theorists intend to assert something stronger than mere logical equivalence—they mean to assert that the reason that an act has the moral property is due to the fact it has the non-moral property. When a moralist asserts (12), it is reasonable to assume that he means to say that *the reason why* an act is morally forbidden is because God forbids it.[21] Typically a moralist intends to explain, by means of a moral principle, why it is that something is MM—and the assertion is that it is MM because it is NM.

Identifying Non-Moral Properties with Moral Properties

There are two reasonable ways to understand a stronger relationship than logical equivalence between the propositions in the consequent of (6). One is the claim that NM and MM are in fact the same property, that the predicates that express them refer to the same property. Sometimes this claim is advanced by arguing that the predicates that express NM and MM are synonymous, and therefore they must refer to the same property. This reasoning is susceptible to the Open Question Argument, as we noted in chapter 2. Recall that the way that argument goes is: suppose a person asserts that "being forbidden by God" and "being morally impermissible" are synonymous; therefore, they refer to the same property. One cannot meaningfully ask the question "this act is forbidden by God, but is it forbidden by God?" but one can meaningfully ask "this act is forbidden by God, but is it morally impermissible?" This latter question is an open question, where

---

21. If one took the alternative reading, that the moralist is saying that God forbids it because it is morally impermissible, then (a) is more about God than about morality. On this way of reading (a), we do not find out why something is morally impermissible, only what it is that God forbids. Plato in the dialogue *Euthyphro* has Socrates make this point. After several efforts to explain what is "pious" (right), Euthyphro finally says it is what all the gods approve. Socrates then asks whether it is pious because it is approved by the gods, or whether the gods approve it because it is pious. Euthyphro chooses the latter, to which Socrates tells him that that answer will not do. Socrates is not interested in why the gods approve something; he is interested in why something is pious. Socrates here typifies a moral philosopher in wanting to know why some things are MP and others are MI. We revisit the problem with Euthyphro's answer to Socrates in chapter 7.

Moral Principles

the earlier one clearly is not. Therefore, the argument goes, "being forbidden by God" and "being morally impermissible" are not synonymous, for if they were then either question would be equally open. This Open Question Argument probably works against claims of synonymy, but such claims are wrong-headed to begin with. The claim that moralists are usually advancing is that the expressions have a common referent—not a common meaning. "The square root of 1296" and "36" are not synonymous, but they refer to the same number. The argument for a claim as serious as that some nonmoral property is identical to some moral property should not be based on something as flimsy and mutable as common semantic meanings.

Suppose someone subscribes to a moral theory like Mill's, except that she holds that the two predicates in her moral principle each refer to the same property. How could she argue for that? As already noted, a good argument cannot be based primarily on what one means when making a moral judgment. A person may simply not know that saying something is morally obligatory means that he is referring to the property *being an act such that there is no other act the agent could do that would have higher utility*. How could he know such a thing without first reading Mill (which so few people have done)? So if one thinks Mill's view is the true view, how could one argue the case?

The way a moral principle regarding acts is developed goes something like this: a philosopher thinks pre-theoretically about those acts that seem pretty clearly to be MI and those that seem pretty clearly to be MP. Then he asks himself, "Which property or properties do those acts that are obviously MI (for instance) have in common, or what property do they all lack?" Or perhaps he examines just one or two clear cases, and asks, "Why is this so clearly MI?" He forms his hypothesis as to the NM that goes along with MI, and tests it against some harder cases. If the hypothesis passes the tests, that is well and good. Perhaps this NM goes along with acts that are MI. If the hypothesis misses on some harder cases, perhaps it can be amended so it works out better. If the hypothesis seems to fit all the clear and harder cases, then the moralist may assume that it will fit the much harder cases. These hardest cases are the ones about which we are the most unsure, and are the reason why we need a moral theory in the first place. Thus the moral theory will help us determine what is MI or is not MI in those difficult cases when our natural moral capacities seem insufficient.

If I have accurately described what a moralist does, then there is little reason for the moralist to think that some moral predicate and some non-moral predicate are referring to the same property. All he can demonstrate is that a moral property and a non-moral property are coextensive, that is, anything that has one of them has the other. If he could go on to make the case that a moral predicate and a non-moral predicate are synonymous, perhaps that would show that they both refer to the same property. But the Open Question Argument is an argument against any possible synonymy between a moral and non-moral predicate. A moralist could, nevertheless, insist that although the predicates are not synonymous, the property referred to by each predicate is identical; thus the propositions that attribute each property to something are coextensive.

It is hard to see how one could argue for such a view, and there is at least some reason to think this is not what a moral theorist intends to assert. If one holds that NM is identical to MM, then it would be theoretically possible to translate moral judgments and precepts into non-moral statements, and so eliminate moral language altogether. After all, if "water" and "H2O" both refer to the same substance, theoretically we could stop using the word "water" and always say "H2O." If NM and MM refer to the same property, and the same example as above, instead of making the moral judgment "Bob did something morally impermissible when he shot the bystander" we could say "Bob did something that God forbids when he shot the bystander." Moral precepts could similarly be translated, for example, "Deceiving others is morally impermissible" becomes "God forbids deceiving others." Thus if some NM is identical to some MM, then every moral judgments could be translated into non-moral statements. This is a significant and troubling outcome. It means that moral speech is just a peculiar way of saying something—a way of speaking, a language game that does not need to be played because it does not add anything to what can be said in other ways. This contradicts the view of Moore and others that moral properties are simple and not reducible, by which he means that they are not identical to any non-moral properties.

Moralists are saying something stronger than logical equivalence when they propose a moral theory—they are attempting to give some explanation for moral propositions. When a moralist asserts a moral principle, he is not merely saying that some moral proposition and some non-moral proposition have the same truth value. Invariably, he is making a stronger claim, that somehow the non-moral property is the basis, or ground, or reason for the moral property. Mill is not simply asserting that *being morally obligatory* and *being an act such that there is no other act the agent could do that would have higher utility* are logically equivalent. He is saying that having the latter property brings about or causes the moral property.

Metacausality

Philosophers grapple with ways of expressing moral principles that are something stronger than mere logical equivalence between NM and MM. For example, in "A Modified Divine Command Theory of Ethical Wrongness" moralist Robert Merrihew Adams starts by stating a simple, unmodified divine command theory. This is the theory that ethical wrongness consists in being contrary to God's commands, or that the word "wrong" in ethical contexts means "contrary to God's commands." It implies that the following two statement forms are logically equivalent. Adams writes:

> (1) It is wrong (for A) to do X.
> (2) it is contrary to God's commands (for A) to do X.
>
> Of course that is not all that the theory implies. It also implies that (2) is conceptually prior to (1), so that the meaning of (1) is to be explained in terms of (2), and not the other way round.[22]

Here Adams makes the point that a divine command moral theory does not merely assert the logical equivalence of two propositions but "implies" that one proposition is conceptually prior and explains the other. What Adams says about this divine command theory can be generalized for every philosophical moral theory. The goal is not only to know how to distinguish what is MM and MC, we also want to know why something is MM. Also, Adams confirms what was stated above, that a moralist takes the non-moral proposition to be conceptually prior to the moral proposition, so that the proposed moral system is explained by, or based on, or depends on, some non-moral property.

Something stronger than logical equivalence is needed to make more clear what moral philosophers are asserting in a moral principle. The problem is that in terms of truth functional logic there is no stronger relationship between two propositions than that of logical equivalence. We need one where one proposition somehow is the basis, or ground, of the other. But what is this grounding relationship? To express what is needed a relationship I will call *metacausality* is required. Metacausality is a relationship

---

22. Adams, "Divine Command," 318–19.

which holds between two states of affairs. Informally, it is the logical equivalence of the propositions expressing the states of affairs plus the notion that one state of affairs brings about, or causes, the other.[23] (The reason that we cannot simply use the word "cause" is because that word is used in connection with physical or event causation, and that is not in view here.)

Using the idea of metacausality, a moral principle has the form:

(13) x is M ↔ (x is NM metacauses that x is MM).[24]

So a stronger view than expressed in (12) is

(14) x is an act ↔ God's forbidding x metacauses that x is morally impermissible.

If we use the symbol "▶" to mean that what is left of the symbol metacauses what is right of the symbol, then (14) becomes

(15) x is an act ↔ God's forbidding x ▶ x is morally impermissible.

This means that God's forbidding x brings it about that it is morally wrong. And it means if any act is morally wrong, God's forbidding it is what makes it so. It explains why x is wrong. A moral principle asserting the stronger relationship which grounds the moral claim, i.e. (15), I call an *explanatory moral principle*, since it not only identifies what has a moral property but also explains why anything has the moral property it does. Since moral philosophers have typically not merely intended to identify what is MP or MI, but also to ground their claim, moral philosophers typically intend to assert an explanatory moral principle.

We have now distinguished three kinds of moral principles: first, there are *moral system principles* that only assert the logical equivalence of *x is NM* and *x is MM* for things in the moral field. The shortcoming of such principles is that they fail to give any explanation why something is MM. They merely identify a necessary link between NM and MM. A second possibility is that there are moral principles that assert that NM is identical to MM for things in the moral field. The problem with this possibility is that these moral principles are stronger than what is needed, hard to argue for, and make the elimination of moral language possible. They say more than

---

23. The technical definition of metacausality is: For any two states of affairs, P and Q, P *metacauses* Q if and only if (1) P brings it about that Q (and not vice versa); and (2) the propositions corresponding to P and Q, viz. (x)Px and (x)Qx, are necessarily logical equivalents.

24. Stated symbolically, (x)((Mx→(NMx ▶ MMx)).

Moral Principles

what most moralist intend to assert. The third type of moral principle, an explanatory moral principle, is what most moralists try to produce.

The Modality of Moral Propositions

A remaining question about moral propositions, and particularly moral principles, has to do with their modality: are they necessary or contingent? According to the semantics of modal logic, a proposition is necessarily true if and only if it is obtains in all possible worlds, and necessarily false if it does not obtain in any possible world. A proposition is contingent if and only if it obtains in some possible worlds, but not in all.[25]

One way of considering this question would be to inquire whether Mill or Kant meant to assert that their moral principles are necessary truths. Did Mill think (1) is necessarily true? Did Kant think (2) is? These questions, although interesting, are not the focus of the present quest. What is of interest for present purposes is what they should have thought about the modality of their moral principles, not what either may have actually thought about them.[26] This latter issue is an historical question.

One reason for thinking a moral principle is necessary is that when someone challenges the truth of a moral principle, he will cite possible examples that call into question the truth of the moral principle. The challenger will identify a hypothetical situation (a possible world) in which the moral principle yields a result that incorrectly attributes the wrong moral property to something in the moral field of the theory. Thus the principle is false—even though the situation presented is hypothetical. Moral principles are supposed to work for possible situations as well as for actual ones. Alan Donagan criticizes rule utilitarianism in "Is There a Credible Form of Utilitarianism?" by claiming that the moral theory would require adopting a rule (Caiaphas's rule) which could result in justifying as morally permissible the intentional killing of an innocent person, say, if such a killing

---

25. A possible world is a maximal set of propositions that are logically consistent. Thus for any proposition p, in each possible world either p or ~p will obtain. For a proposition to "obtain" in a possible world means that it is true in that world. (Necessary propositions that obtain in every possible world are necessarily true; necessary propositions that fail to obtain in any possible world are necessarily false. Propositions that obtain in some, but not all, possible worlds are contingent.)

26. The accuracy of Feldman's formulation of Mill or Kant's moral principles is not our interest here.

would save thousands of lives.[27] Since Donagan believes such a killing is morally impermissible, he believes he has described a possible situation in which rule utilitarianism does not obtain. Thus it is possible that rule utilitarianism is false—which entails that it cannot be necessarily true. This strategy of imagining possible circumstances where a moral principle will misidentify what is MI or MP would seem to require that moral principles are understood to be necessarily true, that is, true in all possible worlds. At least we can see that Donagan—and every other moralist who makes use of hypothetical counter-examples to moral principles—understands moral principles to be more than contingent. Since this strategy of finding possible counter-examples to moral principles (as well as moral precepts) is universally practiced, it seems moralists agree that moral principles are not merely contingent.

Perhaps, then, moral principles are necessary. (The idea of necessity here is broadly logical necessity.)[28] We should not jump to this conclusion too rapidly, however. It has some very significant implications. From one perspective, logical necessity seems too strong a modality for moral principles. Our moral obligations stem in part from the kind of creatures we are and the kind of world we inhabit, but other sorts of worlds are possible. Some possible world, B, could be so dissimilar to this world that human beings in B would have some moral obligations that sound bizarre in the actual world. Imagine that in B whacking a person with a bat is pleasurable for the one whacked, a way of encouraging him that does no lasting physical harm. In B we may be morally obliged to learn how to whack a person more effectively, or to own multiple bats, or to whack others regularly. Each of these would be examples of moral precepts we may have in possible world B. Note that these moral precepts are all for the purpose of encouraging others, they are applications of an even more general moral precept, and that more general moral precept is the same in the actual world and the imagined possible world. The precept *when given the opportunity it is morally permissible to encourage one another* seems to be true in both worlds. Is it true in all possible worlds? Probably not. The pattern seems to be this: that as the precepts encompass more and more of the moral acts, that is, as they become more and more general, they seem to be more and more like

---

27. Donagan, "Utilitarianism" 199. A form of this objection to utilitarianism will resurface in chapter 5, which deals with the moral field.

28. Alvin Plantinga has circumscribed the relevant notion of "broadly logical necessity" in *Nature of Necessity*, 1–9.

Moral Principles

necessary truths. On this analysis, when they reach maximal size, that is, when a precept becomes a moral principle covering the complete moral field, perhaps they approximate broadly logical necessity. Perhaps moral precepts are typically contingent, but moral principles are necessary.

Another better possibility for the modality of moral propositions is a notion borrowed from the logic of counterfactuals. A counterfactual proposition is a conditional "if/then" where the "if" statement is clearly false. In truth functional logic, a false antecedent always makes the entire proposition false. So both of these conditional propositions are false: *if 2+2 is 5, then the square of 3 is 8* and also *if 2+2 is five, then the square of 3 is 9*—if you have a false antecedent, the truth or falsity of the consequent does not matter, the false antecedent makes the conditional sentence false. But conditional sentences in ordinary English are not always understood so strictly. A poor person could assert, "If I have five million dollars, I am no longer poor." Although the antecedent "I have five million dollars" is false, contrary to truth functional logic, the whole assertion seems true. In efforts to understand such propositions, modal logicians use the notion of possible worlds. In particular, they use the idea of proximate possible worlds, that is, possible worlds that are as similar to the actual world as possible in which the antecedent is true. Some antecedents are true in possible worlds that are similar enough to this world for the truth value of the counterfactual claim to be assessed; others open up possible worlds that are so different from the actual world that the truth value of the counterfactual claim is difficult to assess. For example, *If Tom were 8 feet tall and in college, then he would be on his college basketball team* seems like a close enough possible world for us to assess that it is true, but *If New York City was in Mississippi, then the Confederacy would have won the Civil War* is much harder to assess.

So maybe moral principles are not necessarily true, but true in every possible world proximate to the actual world. Perhaps this is also the modality of moral precepts. If we commit to this, we avoid the view that true moral principles are necessarily true, which can run into real problems—especially for moralists who think that the moral order is metacaused by attributes of human nature, but it is possible for these attributes to be quite different than they are in this world. But this view of the modality of morality explains why one can propose counter-examples that are possible, but not actual, to test the truth of a proposed moral principle or precept. The counter-examples that are attempted to disprove a moral principle or precept need to be taken from a possible world proximate to the real world. The moral precept *Lying is morally wrong* is not shown to be false by a counter-example produced in which zebras can talk and are viciously anti-human.[29]

There is no term in the semantics of modal logic for the kind of necessity that extends only to possible worlds proximate to the actual world. Suppose we name it *proximate-world necessity* and say that a proposition is proximate-world necessarily true if and only if it is true in all the possible worlds proximate to the actual world. We must recognize, of course, that the limits of what counts as a proximate world is not perfectly clear. Still, it is a significant advance to recognize true moral precepts and moral principles to have proximate world necessity.

Conclusion

In this chapter I have explained that moral principles are the heart of a moral theory. The logical structure of moral principles involves both identifying the moral field of the theory and distinguishing what has a particular moral property rather than its complement. We have discovered that there are different kinds of moral principles possible including both a moral system principle and an explanatory moral principle. The latter uses a relationship we have identified as metacausality. This relationship is what moralists typically are intending to assert when they link a non-moral property to a moral property in a moral principle. We have also determined that the modality of true moral principles and moral precepts is not merely contingent, nor logically necessary, but something in-between—proximate-world necessity.

---

29. Saying that moral principles are proximate world necessary does not mean that no specific moral precepts are necessary in the broadly logical sense. For example, if God exists then the precept *worshipping God is morally obligatory* is necessarily true in the broadly logical sense.

5

The Moral Field
Distinguishing the Moral and the Amoral

In this chapter we consider the moral field—asking what things, persons, objects, acts, and events can have a moral property. In the previous chapter I identified and elucidated *the field of a moral theory*. A moral theory needs to identify what sorts of "things" have moral properties and what sorts of "things" don't have moral properties.[1] Those things that lack any moral property are *amoral*[2] according to the theory; that is, they fall outside the extension of the theory's moral field.[3] The identity of the moral field of a moral theory is important because it is with respect to it that the moral properties used in the theory are relative complements. So within the theory's moral field, if something lacks being MM, then it is MC.

Identifying the extension of the moral field is one part of what a moral theory does. In this chapter we move from metaethical issues to something that is a part of developing a moral theory. Most moral theorists have not worried too much about the moral field, perhaps because they think it easily characterized. As we will discover, however, identifying what is moral

---

1. For a moral theory c, the field of the theory is the extension of the property M which is used in the moral principle of c.

2. Sometimes a person may use "amoral" to mean "without morality" not in the sense that it is lacking any moral property but in the sense that someone lacks moral sensibility. It is not used in this sense in this work.

3. As explained in previous chapters, "M" denotes the property of being moral (as opposed to amoral). It is not a property variable—it is the maximal property with respect to which MM and MC are relative complements.

(as opposed to amoral) is not so simple. At the outset, there are no obvious reasons to think that distinguishing the moral and the amoral would be any easier than distinguishing what is morally impermissible and what is morally permissible. Since few moralists have systematically addressed the issue of what is in the moral field, I think it is helpful to sketch out the concept and contents of the moral field.

In a well-formed explanatory moral principle a moral theorist identifies the moral field and also identifies a non-moral state of affairs that metacauses a moral state of affairs of something in the moral field. Even a well-formed moral system principle identifies the moral field of the theory. Thus by definition any moral principle identifies what the moralist considers the moral field. Whatever is outside the scope of the moral principle is amoral—outside the field of the moral theory.

The Concept of the Complete Moral Field

Let's begin by considering again Feldman's rendition of Mill's moral principle:

(1) An act is right if and only if there is no other act the agent could have done instead that has a higher utility than it has.

(1) does not make it clear exactly what the moral field of the theory is. It is not in the proper logical form as explained in the previous chapter, and even if it were, it doesn't make clear what counts as an act. But if we take it that this is a moral principle (and not just a general moral precept), then according to it *acts* alone can have moral properties. Anything that is not an act is outside the moral field of this theory and is amoral (on the theory). Sometimes a moral principle is even more vague about the identity of its moral field. For example, consider the poorly formed moral principle:

(2) x is morally obligatory if and only if God commands x.[4]

The moral field is unclear in this example of a moral principle. God has commanded specific act-tokens in the past, and commanded certain act-types more generally. But on the Christian account it was by his command that the cosmos came into being, and all created things are still under his command. So, for instance, by being poorly stated this principle may entail

---

4. Here I use the normal language of material equivalence ("if and only if") rather than the more precise idea of metacausality.

The Moral Field

that the planets are morally obligatory or have moral obligations. Clearly, that is nonsense.

If there is a true and complete moral theory, that is, a theory that accounts for everything that has a moral property, then the moral field of that theory will include everything that is in the moral field and exclude everything that is not in it—everything that is *amoral*. Let's call this whole moral field the *complete moral field*. So the goal of this chapter is to identify the complete moral field which is, of course, the moral field of a true moral theory.[5]

A True Moral Theory and a Complete Moral Field

The complete moral field is the field of a true moral theory. A *true moral theory* is one which does not entail any false propositions. There are two kinds of false propositions possible in a moral system: one which attributes an incorrect moral property to something in the moral field—like entailing that child sacrifice is morally permissible; and another which attributes a moral property to something that is outside the moral field—like saying that horseradish is morally bad. In the sample divine command principle (2) above, the implication that the planets are morally obligatory is another example of the latter kind of error. A *complete moral field* is one which identifies everything that has a moral property and does not include anything that lacks a moral property. A true moral theory attributes the correct moral property to each thing in the complete moral field.[6]

Is There a Complete Moral Field?

Consider first whether this query itself may be mistaken. Perhaps there is no one complete moral field. Perhaps each moral theorist may select or

---

5. Addressing the question as to what is in the complete moral field is important for proposing a moral theory and needed for framing a true moral principle. Identifying the moral field is to understand what a moral theory is a theory of. It comprises a part of the subject matter of moral science.

6. With this definition, it is possible that there is more than one true moral theory. For two moral system principles could entail all the same moral judgments while entailing different but true non-moral propositions. But any moral system principle which entails any false proposition, by itself or in conjunction with any other true propositions, is false. Any true and complete moral theory will entail all and only true moral judgments, and will entail only true non-moral propositions.

utilize a moral field of any extension. Moral expressivists deny that anything has any moral property, so on their view there is no moral field.[7] Even moral realists use different moral fields, so perhaps it is a mistake to try to identify the one moral field. Maybe moral fields are more like baseball parks than football fields. The former may vary considerably in size and configuration, while the latter are always the same dimensions. Perhaps moral fields are always relative to some moral theory and there is no one complete moral field.

However, there is reason to think there is one complete moral field. Imagine a moral principle that identifies *acts done on Tuesdays* as the moral field. Such a principle would be hard to take seriously because immediately one recognizes this theory cannot be complete. How do we know that? Simply because everyone recognizes that some things other than acts done on Tuesdays can have moral properties. Some things do have a moral property (like assassinating Anwar Sadat) and some things lack a moral property (like the number seven). Some things must be in the moral field and some things must be excluded. So a moral theorist may be mistaken when he tries to identify the moral field. He may have a moral theory in which the moral field only includes integers or acts done on Tuesdays. A moral theory may imply that something is amoral that is in fact in the moral field; for instance, it could fail to take the assassination of Anwar Sadat as being in the moral field. Or a moral theory could imply that something is in the moral field that is in fact amoral, perhaps entailing that sparrows are morally bad. So the moral field of a moral theory may be identical to the complete moral field, or it may be a proper subset of it, or it may include something that is amoral, or it is even possible there may be no intersection between the moral field of a theory and the complete moral field (although in such a case it would be hard to recognize it as a moral theory).

What this shows is that we all have some grasp of how to use moral predicates and the sorts of subjects to which they can be *literally* attributed. But this isn't just a question of knowing how to use language. The reason we know how to link some subjects and moral predicates is that we understand the sorts of things that have moral properties and those that do not. This understanding is not exact—our understanding of the idea of what is in the moral field is a bit blurry on the edges, yet for the most part we know the sorts of things that belong in it. In this chapter I attempt to make this blurry idea as clear as possible.

7. For example, A. J. Ayer calls any moral property a "pseudo-concept."

The Moral Field

Moral Properties and the Moral Field

The moral field is comprised of everything that has a moral property. In chapter 3 we saw that there are seven common moral predicates that express five moral properties. Recall that the seven most commonly used moral predicates are "is morally right," "is morally wrong," "is morally permissible," "is morally impermissible," "is morally obligatory," "is morally good, and "is morally bad." I pointed out in chapter 3 that "is morally wrong" and "is morally impermissible" express the same moral property. In addition, "is morally right" is ambiguous. It can express either the same property that is expressed by "is morally permissible" or "is morally obligatory." Thus *"it is morally right to pay one's taxes"* can mean either that *it is morally permissible to pay one's taxes* (a relatively weak assertion) or that *it is morally obligatory to pay one's taxes* (a much stronger assertion). Since the predicate "is morally right" is ambiguous, it is preferable to avoid using it and instead to use either "is morally permissible" or "is morally obligatory," depending on which property is intended. So we are left with five moral properties. Whatever can have one of these five properties is in the moral field. These five properties divide neatly into two groups: *being morally permissible, being morally impermissible,* and *being morally obligatory* are in the first group, and *being morally good* and *being morally bad* are in the second group.

The Two Sets of Moral Properties

The mutual analyzability of the relative complements *being morally good* and *being morally bad* is straightforward. Whatever is in the moral field and is not morally good is morally bad, and whatever is in the moral field and is not morally bad is morally good.

In ordinary English usage, a person who claims an act is morally obligatory is claiming that the act is required. An act that is required must also be morally permissible. One could say that a morally obligatory act is morally permissible and more, it is required (obligatory). Strictly speaking, an act's being morally obligatory is a special case of its being morally permissible.[8] Because of this overlap between the extension of the property of

---

8. As stated in chapter 3, it would be helpful if we had a term for the moral property of those acts that are neither morally obligatory nor morally impermissible, acts that are morally permissible *simpliciter*. But there is no such term. This problem with moral

being morally obligatory and *being morally permissible*, it is most convenient to express moral principles in terms of the relative complements *being morally permissible* and *being morally impermissible*.

Being morally permissible, being morally impermissible and *being morally obligatory* can all be understood in terms of each other. Thus we can analyze *being morally obligatory* and *being morally impermissible* in terms of *being morally permissible*. First, anything in the moral field that is not morally permissible is morally impermissible.[9] Second, if something is morally permissible, and it is not morally permissible to fail to do it, it is morally obligatory. We can also analyze *being morally permissible* and *being morally obligatory* in terms of *being morally impermissible*. First, anything in the moral field that is not morally impermissible is morally permissible. Second, if something is not morally impermissible and it is not morally permissible to fail to do it, then it is morally obligatory to do it. Lastly, we can analyze *being morally permissible* and *being morally impermissible* in terms of *being morally obligatory*. First, anything in the moral field that is morally obligatory not to do is morally impermissible. Second, anything in the moral field which is neither morally obligatory to do nor morally obligatory not to do is morally permissible.

This analysis, however, does not account for everything in the moral field. Not everything in the moral field is either morally permissible or morally impermissible—for instance, a *person* is neither. And not everything in the moral field is morally good or morally bad—*act-tokens* are neither.[10] An act-token like *Rose's shopping last Monday at Target* is neither morally good nor morally bad, however it is morally permissible or morally impermissible. So the two sets of moral properties seem to indicate that the moral field has two major extensions. The first extension is that of *being*

---

terms and properties is paralleled in metaphysics by the modal terms "possible" and "necessary." In ordinary English a state of affairs that is necessary is, of course, possible. But in technical contexts where modal issues are discussed, it is important to distinguish what is necessary and what is merely possible. Metaphysicians have the advantage of a vocabulary that includes "necessary" and "contingent," and *x is contingent* entails *x is not necessary*. Thus there is available a way of speaking of which makes the same distinction without violating ordinary English use. Sadly, there is no term that functions like "contingent" for "morally permissible."

9. Obviously anything that that is not morally permissible lacks that property. So the number eight and rabbits lack that property, yet they are not thereby morally impermissible. Moral permissibility and impermissibility are relative complements with respect to things in the moral field.

10. Act-tokens are either morally permissible or morally impermissible.

an act-token, which divides the moral field into that which is morally permissible and that which is morally impermissible. The second extension is divided into that which is morally good and that which is morally bad; this second extension is more difficult to characterize briefly. We could posit that that there are actually two different moral fields for what is morally good and what is morally bad, namely, persons and states of affairs. In that case there would be three moral fields: act-tokens, persons, and states of affairs. These distinct moral fields can be seen in some of the moral theories that have been advanced. Some moral principles are expressed in terms of act-tokens, as we have seen in Mill and Kant; other theories are about the morality of certain states of affairs, for example, the maximal net pleasure (that is, pleasure minus pain) possible in a specific situation. G. E. Moore develops his moral theory in terms of states of affairs he identifies as morally good. Still other moral theories are virtue theories that are expressed in terms of morally good and morally bad persons. So some moral principles may take act-tokens as the moral field, others take persons, and still others take states of affairs.[11]

Mutuality

These three options for moral principles generate a problem, if we assume that moral properties can be literally predicated of three kinds of things. Then any theory that only deals with one set of things in the moral field cannot be a complete moral theory, as there will be a lot of members of the true moral field about which it will be silent. A moral theory that attempts to explain what metacauses things being morally good may miss what makes an act morally permissible; and a moral theory that attempts to explain what metacauses acts being morally impermissible may miss what makes a person, say, morally good. That is, we have a problem of incompleteness,

---

11. The moral property *being morally good* may be thought to suffer from the same ambiguity problem as *being morally right*, but we do not have the same easy correction of an alternative way to express them. "Being morally good" can mean either something like "is morally acceptable" or it may mean "is morally exemplary." But there is no standard way to express this difference. If we had three moral properties—being morally acceptable, being morally exemplary, and being morally bad—it would be easier to expand the moral field so that, for instance, all states of affairs would have one of these three properties, with the vast majority being morally acceptable. As it is, however, we will discover that many states of affairs don't seem to be either morally good or morally bad and so are not in the moral field.

unless there is a way of explicating the relationship between these three moral fields so that any one has implications for the other ones.

In what follows I will show how moral statements attributing *being morally good* (or *being morally bad*) to something can be unpacked into logically equivalent assertions attributing *being morally permissible* (or *being morally impermissible*) to some act-tokens. If this analysis is successful, then any moral principle that uses persons or states of affairs can be expressed by an equivalent one that has act-tokens as its moral field. This would indirectly support the assumption of many moralists that the subject matter of ethics is human conduct.[12]

Even if the analysis below is sound, it does not imply that *being morally good* and *being morally bad* are dispensable. I attempt to show how moral principles using *being morally good* and *being morally bad* imply assertions about *being morally permissible* and *being morally impermissible*. I find the analysis of *being morally permissible* in terms of *being morally good* less satisfying and appealing than the reverse, because the moral field composed of persons or some states of affairs seems messier than a moral field composed simply of act-tokens. However, the analysis is possible in either direction. If I am successful in showing how this goes, it will demonstrate that each set of moral properties has implications involving moral properties from the other set. This mutuality among moral properties reveals an internal simplicity and coherence to moral reality.

In the process of showing this mutuality, I will introduce the idea of *field conversion principles* that show how these analyses can be done in general. If I succeed, then it will turn out that a moralist can use either a moral property from the group *being morally impermissible, being morally obligatory, or being morally permissible,* or use one of *being morally good* or *being morally bad,* and still have a complete moral field and a true moral theory.

Understanding Moral Goodness and Badness

What sorts of things can be literally morally good or morally bad? Some of the difficulty in answering this question stems from using the predicates

---

12. Alan Donagan writes that traditional morality is "the standard by which systems of mores, actual and possible, are to be judged and by which everybody ought to live, no matter what the mores of his neighbors may be," in Donagan, *Theory of Morality*, 1. Henry Stob writes, "Ethics is the study of the voluntary conduct of individual man " in Stob, *Ethical Reflections*, 13.

"is good" and "is bad" in multiple contexts and can refer to several different properties—not just moral ones. (Thus the wisdom in using the whole predicate "is *morally* good" and the like to make moral propositions.) People speak of good students, good movies, and good friends. In none of these cases are they attributing moral goodness.

Sometimes statements that refer to moral properties need to be unpacked to see exactly what has the property. We saw this in chapter 2 and 3 when I explained that moral precepts have act-types as their subject and seem to attribute a moral property to them. But act-types themselves are not acts, they are a kind or type of act. Since they are not acts, they are not in the moral field. Since they are not in the moral field they cannot have any moral property. The moral precept "Telling a lie is morally impermissible" does not mean that the act-type *telling a lie* has the property of being morally impermissible—even though that is what it looks like initially. What it means is that any act-token that is an instance of telling lies has the property of being morally impermissible. Sometimes the way we speak is misleading unless it is unpacked correctly.

Persons

We frequently attribute moral properties to persons, and not just to the acts they do. Virtue ethics attempts to explain what makes a person morally good or virtuous, and what makes a person morally bad or vicious. Addressing such issues systematically is worthwhile and important. Clearly a person can be morally good or bad. But on what basis is a person morally good or morally bad?

Let's consider some of these beginning with a clear case, attributing *being morally good* to an individual person.

(A) Dexter is a morally good man.

What does this mean, exactly? Would we say it of Dexter if he is comatose and has been since birth? No, clearly not, but why not? Is it not because attributing moral goodness to a person implies something about that person's past, present, and future conduct? Aristotle said, "Virtue is only known by its acts."[13] What does (A) imply about the act-tokens of which Dexter is the agent? Initially, it seems there are three ways to understand (A) in terms of

---

13. Aristotle, *Nicomachean Ethics* I.8. This is an epistemological observation, not an ontological one.

the act-tokens of which Dexter is the moral agent. One strong interpretation is

(B) No act-token of which Dexter is the moral agent is morally impermissible.

If (B) is the right way to unpack (A), then if (A) is true, then every act-token that Dexter does is morally permissible (remember, this may include what is morally obligatory). This is a pretty strong claim—impossible for Dexter or anyone to live up to. We often say someone is a morally good person even if we know she has told some lies, or done something else that is morally impermissible. So we should weaken (B).

(C) Very few of the act-tokens of which Dexter is the moral agent are morally impermissible.

But even (C) is too strong. Suppose in almost every respect Dexter avoids doing anything that is morally impermissible, but that Dexter has committed several murders. In that case, (C) could be true and (A) would be false. So (C) is not the right way to unpack (A). We need to qualify and limit the kinds of act-tokens that Dexter does. There are various ways of doing this.

(D) Dexter is the agent of fewer and less serious act-tokens that are morally impermissible than most persons.

If it turns out the Dexter has murdered someone, then both (D) and (A) would be false. If Dexter only does a few run-of-the-mill act-tokens that are morally impermissible, like breaking a minor promise, or telling a minor lie, then both (D) and (A) are true. Now we may want to supplement Dexter's character with the regular performance of act-tokens which are morally obligatory for him, and also indicate that he is disposed toward such.

(E) Dexter is the agent of fewer and less serious act-tokens that are morally impermissible and is less disposed toward doing them than most persons, and he consistently performs and is more disposed toward doing those act-tokens which are morally obligatory.

When someone says (A) what they attribute to Dexter is more explicitly expressed in (E). Perhaps even (A) and (E) are logical equivalents, and even if they are not, it is hard to see that there is not some variation of (E) that would be the logical equivalent of (A), even if it is difficult to state exactly. If this is right, then a statement like (A) about a person that uses *being morally good* is logically equivalent to some statement that only uses morally permissible, morally impermissible, and/or morally obligatory.

The Moral Field

Now let us consider more closely the relationship between (A) and (E). As we saw in chapter 4, even when two propositions are logically equivalent we can ask whether the state of affairs expressed by one metacauses the state of affairs expressed by the other. So the question is whether (A) and (E) are metacausally related, and if so, whether (A) metacauses (E) or (E) metacauses (A).

When a person is asked to give a character reference, the inquiry normally includes questions like: how long have you known the person? What is the nature of your relationship with the person? The purpose of such questions is so that the inquirer has an idea of the level of familiarity the one giving the recommendation has with the sort of conduct in which the person engages. What needs to be understood is whether this level of familiarity with the person's act-tokens is sufficient to make a generalization about his or her character. This indicates that a statement about a person's character is a generalization about the act-tokens the person typically does (or avoids). So it seems that (E) metacauses (A); that is, (E) explains (A) in a way that (A) does not explain (E).[14]

Given this analysis, note that if Dexter is a morally good man, we can learn what is likely to be morally permissible by observing what Dexter does. If it is true that *Dexter is a good man*, then by watching what act-tokens Dexter does we can learn what is most likely morally permissible. But it is clearly false that Dexter's doing some act-token is what *makes* it morally permissible. In fact, should Dexter do something morally impermissible, it counts as evidence that he is not morally good. What makes an act-token morally permissible is an ontological issue; watching Dexter to find out what is morally permissible is an epistemological strategy. Dexter may consistently do act-tokens that are morally permissible, and so we may uncover what act-tokens are morally permissible by observing Dexter, but even if Dexter is an exceptionally morally good person, the act-tokens he does do not become morally permissible because Dexter does them, rather his consistency in doing them is how we know that he is morally good. Aristotle, a virtue ethicist *par excellence*, said, "By doing the acts that we do in our transactions with other men we become just and good . . . Thus in one word, states of character arise out of like activities."[15] The moral properties

---

14. This illustration shows how it may be more foundational to explain the moral goodness or badness of persons in terms of act-tokens rather than vice versa.

15 Aristotle, *Nicomachean Ethics* II.2.1103b.

of the act-tokens a person does are the basis on which a person is morally good or morally bad.

It turns out, then, that saying that someone is a good person or a bad person can be understood as an abbreviated way of saying something about the number and quality of the impermissible acts that the person had avoided (or done) and or is disposed to avoid (or to do), and the consistency with which the person has done morally obligatory acts. A person really can have the property of *being morally good* or *being morally bad*, but those moral properties can be analyzed into other moral properties having to do with act-tokens.

Animals

What about moral attributions to animals or the behavior of animals? Few people would ascribe moral properties to worms, a few might to tigers, and perhaps many would to their pets. When someone says, "Lassie is a good dog," it seems to parallel "Dexter is a good man." But does it—can Lassie have a moral property? Expressions like these actually are about the behavior of Lassie, like not biting people, not barking too much, and being house broken. In other words, Lassie is behaving the way a human person wants. She is behaving according to human preferences for this dog, and maybe all dogs. She is not both good and a dog; she is a good dog; that is, she exhibits the kind of dog behavior humans prefer. If a person acted like Lassie, having learned to not bite people, to not bark, and being house broken, etc., we would not say he is good, or that he is a good person, or that he is a good dog. We would consider him troubled. What makes a dog good is exhibiting behavior humans prefer for dogs; what makes a human good is exhibiting human, or moral, goodness.

What this suggests is that morality has to do with *being human*. We watch a film of a crocodile lunging at and grasping a wildebeest at the river's edge, and maybe we feel some sympathy for the wildebeest's plight. But is the crocodile acting immorally? It seems not; it is acting according to its nature. Ethics addresses questions like "What is a good human?" "What acts do good human persons do, and which ones do they avoid doing?" Or "Who is a bad person?" A moral theory is one that proposes answers to these and similar questions; it is not about the behavior of animals.[16]

16. This means that mosquitoes are not immoral, and when one has bitten you it has not done anything *morally* wrong.

The Moral Field

Things: Objects and Events

Now let's briefly consider whether objects or events are the kinds of things about which one can literally say, "this is morally good" or "this is morally bad." If so, our next question is whether such an assertion can be unpacked in terms of morally impermissible or morally permissible act-tokens.[17] My analysis leads to the view that neither natural objects, nor human artifacts, nor natural events are in the true moral field.

We begin with human artifacts, because if they are not in the moral field then natural objects are not either. A person may say, "that was a good dinner" or "that was a good movie" or "this is a good chair," but is it conceivable that they are attributing *being morally good* to such things? Can a dinner itself be morally good? Perhaps it is nutritious and perfectly suited to the appetites of those for whom it is prepared. But being nutritious and being well suited to eaters are prudential evaluations or perhaps even aesthetic evaluations. If a person feeds a starving family, and does so at great personal cost, we may be inclined to say that providing and serving the food was morally good, but this is about an act of providing and serving, not the food itself. In such a case the moral judgment would be unpacked so that the event act-token of providing the food to people in need was morally permissible or morally obligatory.

Let's consider another human artifact—can, say, a movie be morally good? If so, can that be analyzed in terms of its relationship to act-tokens? Imagine a movie that instills in most viewers the desire to become morally responsible persons; for example, let's suppose that *An Inconvenient Truth* motivates its viewers to reduce their carbon footprints. Were this the case, would this make the movie itself morally good? I think not. Watching movies may affect viewers, but that is insufficient to place them in the moral field. Human artifacts, and natural ones as well, should not be understood as being morally good or bad. Of course, they can be aesthetically good or bad; a dinner, for example, can be good or bad by some culinary standard. A movie can be produced by a greedy person, directed by a lustful person, have morally bad actors, be full of scenes depicting impermissible

---

17. Sometimes people will use the word "moral" as an adjective to indicate the seriousness of the good or evil about which they are speaking, but this use is not relevant to ethics. To say that natural disasters, death, and disease are not in the moral field is not to diminish their importance or significance. I will argue that both physical objects and natural events are amoral and lie outside the moral field.

act-tokens, have the effect on some people of encouraging them to do impermissible act-tokens and still be an aesthetically good movie.

In general, the conclusion to be drawn is that attributing a moral property to a human artifact is either conflating a moral claim with an aesthetic claim, or is a non-literal, abbreviated way of speaking. In the latter case it is a way of saying that the event act-token resulting in some artifact is morally permissible (or morally impermissible). Saying "is morally good" (or "is morally bad") is often an abbreviated way of summarizing the net moral value of a pattern of event act-tokens. In the case of the movie, saying it is morally good may be a shorthand way of saying that it is conducive to encouraging agents to perform fewer impermissible acts, or it may be a claim about the morality of the act-tokens undertaken by the producer or director in making it. In neither case is the movie itself literally morally good. There are other examples of human artifacts that we could consider, but it is hard to see how they would fare any differently. Thus the conclusion we must draw is that neither natural products nor human artifacts are in the moral field.

Are some natural events in the moral field? Consider some asteroid being pulled into a black hole or the death of a star. Are these events with moral properties? It seems not. Natural events that have little or no impact on human life do not seem to be in the moral field. What about natural events that have an impact on human life? Do these have moral properties? Consider a tornado that devastates a school and kills some children. This would be a tragedy and clearly an evil. Philosophers distinguish between natural evil and moral evil, the former being things that happen without human agency, like tornadoes, tsunamis, earthquakes, illnesses and other natural disasters with harmful effects. A moral evil is an evil that is done by human agents, and refers to the particularly harmful effects of some person's doing a morally impermissible event act-token. But it seems very odd to think that tornadoes are morally bad. We lament the onset of pancreatic cancer in a friend, and we may consider it unfair, but there doesn't seem to be any immorality involved. We say, "It is terrible that John has cancer" and feel some real sadness. It seems there are all kinds of events that we wish not to happen which can have tragic, sad effects on persons. We would say that such events are evil, perhaps, but strictly speaking they are not *morally bad*.[18]

---

18. The predicate "is evil" has both a moral and a non-moral sense. The moral sense of the predicate is a way of attributing morally impermissible to the act-token(s) that

The Moral Field
States of Affairs

Finally, we need to consider states of affairs and ask whether any of them are in the moral field. A state of affairs is expressed by a proposition, thus *it rained in Hoboken on July 2, 1883* expresses the state of affairs of its raining in Hoboken on July 2, 1883. Every proposition expresses a state of affairs— a true proposition expresses an actual state of affairs. We can speak of the moral property that a possible state of affairs would have were it to be an actual state of affairs.[19] So the moral order helps us when we ask whether, say, telling Sally a lie about Tom would be morally permissible before anyone does it.

Some states of affairs seem to have either the moral property of being morally good or being morally bad. For instance, *a serial murderer has been apprehended* seems to be a morally good thing, as would *researchers have discovered a cure for sickle cell anemia,* were it to be actual. Alternatively, *a serial murderer killed another victim* seems to be a morally bad state of affairs. These examples suggest the sort of states of affairs that are in the moral field. Not only does this idea have some intuitive appeal, as seen in the examples, but certain kinds of moral theories require that some states of affairs are in the moral field.

According to teleological moral theories, some states of affairs must be in the moral field. Teleological theories assume that certain states of affairs are morally good (or bad), and analyze what it is for an act-token to be morally permissible or impermissible depending on its causal relationship to these states of affairs.[20] For example, in *Principia Ethica*, G. E. Moore analyzes *being morally obligatory* in terms of moral goodness. "Our 'duty,' therefore, can only be defined as that action which will cause more good to exist in the universe than any possible alternative. And what is 'right' or 'morally permissible' only differs from this, as what will not cause less good than any possible alternative."[21]

A teleological theory will identify some morally good (or morally bad) state of affairs and say that the act-tokens that contribute to actualizing that state of affairs are morally permissible or morally obligatory. So, for

caused it.

19. In proximate possible worlds, as explained in chapter 4.

20. Utilitarian theories are the most common variety of teleological theory.

21. Moore, *Principia Ethica*, 148. It is not until chapter 5 of this work that G. E. Moore first considers what a morally right act is.

example, a hedonist may hold the view that *a human's experiencing pleasure is a morally good state of affairs,* and affirm a moral principle such as

> An act-token is morally permissible if and only if it contributes to some humans experiencing pleasure that exceeds any pain caused.

So certain moral theories require that at least some states of affairs are in the moral field. If a state of affairs is in the moral field it is either morally good (MG) or morally bad (MB).

What distinguishes the states of affairs in the moral field from those which are not in the moral field is difficult to say precisely. Those which are morally good seem to be those that are beneficial to human well-being in some significant way, and those that are morally bad harm human well-being in a significant way. Admittedly this is not a clear way of identifying exactly which states of affairs are in the moral field. At this point, however, that is not important. What is important to recognize is that some states of affairs are in the moral field.

We began this section wondering whether states of affairs are in the moral field, and it seems that some of them are. States of affairs and persons in the moral field are either morally good or morally bad. Earlier we recognized that the moral field composed of acts are either morally permissible or morally impermissible. So now we see clearly that there are two distinct extensions of the moral field, one identified by being either morally good or morally bad (persons and states of affairs) and the other identified by being either morally permissible or morally impermissible (acts). So is the moral order needed to distinguish what is MG and MB, or is it needed to distinguish what is MP and MI, or does it do both?

As promised earlier, this question can be answered by showing how these two different fields are logically related. When a moral principle uses one field, we can see what implications it has for the other field. What is needed are what I call *field conversion principles.* With such principles we can draw the implications a moral principle has for the complete moral field.

Field Conversion Principles

Moral theories traditionally have been distinguished into two kinds: teleological and deontological. Teleological theories identify morally good states of affairs or morally good persons and generate moral precepts based on which acts would bring about these moral goods. Deontological theories identify morally permissible and impermissible acts directly, without regard to the production of what is morally good. Thus the actual basis for the distinction between these two kinds of moral theories involves both the moral properties used and what is in the moral field of the theories.

Thus there are two candidates for the moral field. This is an inelegant outcome. If not resolved it means a moral theory of either kind is incomplete. A deontological moral theory may explain the conditions under which an act is morally obligatory, but it does not tell us which states of affairs are morally good or morally bad. Similarly, a teleological theory may lay out what states of affairs are morally good or morally bad, but it does not always make clear which acts are morally permissible or impermissible. What we need is a way of translating teleological theories into deontological ones, and vice versa. The way this can be done is with field conversion principles. But before explaining what these may look like, consider two reasons why there must be something like field conversion principles.

First, Aristotle stated that one of the ways we identify a science is by its subject matter, and if the moral field constitutes what Aristotle meant by a science's subject matter, then moral theories with completely different fields should not be identifiable as being theories in the same science. But theories which differ in this way are of the same science. From this it follows, given that the subject matter of a science is its field, that both acts and states of affairs constitute the subject matter of moral science. If that is the case, however, then any moral system which takes either one of these and not the other as its field, as most moral theories do, must be incomplete. The only way to escape this untenable conclusion is to recognize that moral claims regarding acts and those regarding states of affairs are mutually analyzable. Such analyses involve the common acceptance of something like field conversion principles.

A second reason for the existence of field conversion principles could be developed from the fact that moral theories with different moral fields are regularly interpreted as conflicting. The possibility of this requires that interpreters employ some principles which translate a moral judgment made about an act into one made about a state of affairs, or vice versa.

The best evidence for thinking that there are such principles which are commonly accepted and operate regularly in our moral thinking is to produce them or at least plausible candidates for them. The importance of these principles is not simply to better understand the structure of moral systems, but also to recognize that both acts and states of affairs/persons can serve as the moral field of a theory. If the moral implications of a moral principle with one field can be drawn for the members of the other moral field, then a moral principle using either field may be complete.

We have already seen that there are some strategies of analysis that allow us to see the implications that one kind of theory may have for another kind of theory. For example, earlier we saw how we could explain what a morally good person is in terms of act-tokens. This means that a virtue theory, which has a moral field of persons, can be converted into a theory about acts. We can use that analysis to generate the first field conversion principle we need.

> (FCPa) A person is good insofar as s/he avoids doing impermissible acts and consistently does morally obligatory acts. A bad person is one who is not a good person.

The field conversion principle by which we can convert a moral theory about persons into a theory about acts is a bit trickier. It would be something this:

> (FCPb) An act is morally impermissible if a morally good person avoids doing it, and an act is morally obligatory if every morally good person does it consistently.

Now we need two additional field conversion principles. One explains how to convert a moral principle that has act-tokens as its moral field to cover states of affairs; and the other explains the reverse conversion. The former of these is something like this:

> (FCPc) States of affairs are morally good or morally bad insofar as they are the consequence of morally permissible or morally impermissible act-tokens, respectively, and/or as they are conducive to the performance of morally permissible or morally impermissible act-tokens, respectively.

By (FCPc) if we know that state of affairs A comes about as a result of someone's morally permissible act-token, and/or A is conducive to the performance of morally permissible act-tokens by moral agents, then A is a morally good state of affairs. This principle, or one very much like it, makes it possible to see the implications for states of affairs for a moral system whose field is act-tokens.

A principle which relates acts to states of affairs is sometimes used, as we have seen in the case of Moore.

The Moral Field

(FCPd) An act is morally permissible insofar as it causes a state of affairs to be brought about which is no less good than any other state of affairs which the agent could have brought about. An act is morally impermissible insofar is it brings about a state of affairs which is less good than some other state of affairs which the agent could have brought about.

The claim is simply that with (FCPa), (FCPb), (FCPc), and (FCPd) we have plausible candidates for those principles which moralists could use in order to see the implications for the complete moral field even when only persons, states of affairs, or acts are used in a moral theory. Thus by using field conversion principles a moral theory which only specifically identifies the moral field as persons, or act-tokens, or states of affairs as the moral field of the theory can be understood to cover the complete moral field.

This all may seem to be a bit makeshift, and the field conversion principles above may not be precisely the best way to convert the field of a moral theory, but they are important to show a way in which a serious problem can be solved. There are two sets of moral properties each of which applies to different kinds of things, and if ethics is one science and not two or three, we must have some way of relating what is morally good to what is morally obligatory, and what is morally bad to what is morally impermissible.

Moral Acts

I conclude the consideration of the moral field by looking at the properties that an act needs to have in order to be in the moral field. One complication that we need to be aware of is a result of how we express moral precepts. We encountered this in chapter 2 when discussing moral language. If someone says, "Telling lies is morally impermissible" it seems he is attributing the property of *being morally impermissible* to the subject of the sentence, the act-type telling lies. But it would be a mistake to analyze his statement this way. The correct way to understand what he has said is that he is attributing being morally impermissible to each act-token that falls under the act-type *telling lies*. An act-type itself is just a property, and since properties are amoral, act-types are outside the moral field. Technically what he says unpacks to mean "Any instance of telling a lie is morally wrong." So moral predicates sometimes appear to be attributing a moral property to something, but things are not always as they seem and it may need some unpacking to see exactly what is being asserted. Here, as with any philosophical issue, how language is used is at best an amateur guide into ontology.

We need to trace in broad outline the difference between human doings that are amoral and human acts which are moral. Some may wish to argue that the term "act" is or should be defined in such a way that it is necessarily the case that all acts are in the moral field. The problem this approach introduces, however, is that there is no unanimity as to what constitutes an act. In common speech the term "act" is used broadly. As a result one can hear of "animal acts," "involuntary acts," and even "non-voluntary acts." Philosophers too hold varying views as to which events are acts. Our question is "what is a moral act?" or, more precisely, "which act-tokens are in the moral field?" The case will be made that to be in the moral field an act-token must be voluntary and purposive.

Voluntary

While it is true that a moralist need not assume any particular analysis or theory regarding (human) acts in order to present a moral system, there is one sort of analysis of acts which should be avoided—those which deny that any human acts are voluntary, such as philosophical behaviorism. Such a theory of acts produces the unfortunate result that the agents of morally permissible acts cannot be praiseworthy and that the agents of morally impermissible acts are not culpable. Rather the kind of acts that are in the moral field must be voluntary. The claim that all moral acts are voluntary has been stated, argued, and defended thoroughly by Alan Gewirth in *Reason and Morality*. Concerning the relevant notion of voluntariness he writes:

> For human behaviors or movements to be actions in the strict sense and hence voluntary or free, certain causal conditions must be fulfilled. Negatively, the behaviors must not occur from one or more of the following kinds of cause: (a) direct compulsion, physical or psychological, by someone or something external to the person; (b) causes internal to the person, such as reflexes, ignorance, or disease, that decisively contribute, in ways beyond his control, to the occurrence of the behavior; (c) indirect compulsion whereby the person's choice to emit the behavior is forced by someone else's coercion. Positively, the person must control his behavior by his own unforced and informed choice. This does not mean that

The Moral Field

whenever he chooses to do something he does it, for he may be unable to do it. It means rather that when his behavior is voluntary or free, his unforced and informed choice is the necessary and sufficient condition of the behavior. For all behaviors that are the objects of moral and other practical precepts, it is assumed that the persons addressed can control their behaviors in this way.[22]

Gewirth's description of voluntariness distinguishes between forces that restrict freedom and the positive control a moral agent must have if his act is moral, the result of a free and informed choice. The forces that restrict freedom can be external or internal. External constraints are forms of compulsion or coercion, and internal constraints are factors like ignorance and disease. This is a narrow view of what a voluntary act is. On Gewirth's view, if a gunman says to Smith "your money or your life," Smith's choice is forced and thus not voluntary in the relevant sense. As a result, on Gewirth's view, such forced choices are "not acts in the strict sense."[23]

The problem with this view can be seen if we imagine a man Smith, with $5 in his wallet, choosing not to give the gunman his money, with the result that he is shot and killed. Was Smith's act a morally permissible choice or not? On Gewirth's view his behavior is not, strictly speaking, an act; it is not in the moral field. But this cannot be right. Smith had at least two choices and he did make a decision to act. Perhaps both choices were morally permissible. Perhaps one of them was morally impermissible and the other morally obligatory. A moral theory should help us sort out the moral implications of just such forced choices rather than say that Smith's choice was not in the moral field because it was a forced choice.

What is needed is a brief way of capturing the relevant notion of voluntariness. Alvin Plantinga provides a clear condition for an act to be voluntary. A voluntary act is one an agent is free to do or to not do. An agent is free with respect to an action if "no causal laws and antecedent conditions determine either that he will perform the action, or that he will not."[24] To be free with respect to an act is a necessary condition of doing the

---

22. Gewirth, *Reason and Morality*, 31.

23. Gewirth is interested in the generic features of acts which will provide him with the justificatory basis of his supreme principle of morality. His intent is not first of all to delimit the moral field. Nevertheless, if his supreme moral principle is derived from the general features of acts, then it will apply only to those acts which have such features. So he is delimiting his moral field, albeit not as such.

24. Plantinga, *Nature of Necessity*, 166.

act voluntarily because at any time a person is free with respect to numerous acts that he does not choose to do.

> (Definition of a voluntary act) A voluntary act e is one which is performed by an agent who is free with respect to e. An agent C is free with respect to an act e if and only if it is within his power to either do e or refrain from doing e.

On this account, Smith's decision to not give $5 to the gunman is a voluntary act. He could have given the money—there are no causal laws or antecedent conditions that determine that he would make the choice not to give it. Contrary to Gewirth, Smith's decision is an act in the sense relevant to morality—that is, it is in the moral field. His choice was powerfully influenced by his options, but he still had the power to do one or the other.

Purposive

Besides being voluntary, each act in the moral field is *purposive*. Gewirth explains what this means:

> In choosing to perform some definite action, the agent must more or less clearly envisage that action: he must know what action it is that he is choosing to perform; that is, he must intend that action in the sense of having it more or less in view and wanting to perform it. He must intend it, moreover, either for its own sake or for the sake of some consequence he wants to achieve by the action, or both. Thus intention or purpose, in the sense of the desired content of an action, is the other side of the control and choice that constitute voluntariness of freedom and that are concerned with bringing about that desired content.[25]

According to Gewirth, acts which are purposive have two features: the conative and the substantive. The first requires that the agent of a moral act is aiming to achieve some goal or purpose by the act (even if on occasion it is done habitually without specific conscious attention to any aim), sometimes the goal is simply the performance of the act itself. The second feature required is that the agent intends to do what he in fact does. Of course it is often the case that the agent of an act intends to achieve some end D by setting in motion a causal sequence of events by the performance of some act A. Gewirth is not claiming under the substantive aspect of purposiveness

---

25. Gewirth, *Reason and Morality*, 38–39.

that D must be achieved before A is purposive. It is enough that A itself was achieved. In general,

> (Definition of a purposive act) An act A is *purposive* if and only if the agent of A performs it in order to achieve some goal, even if that goal is simply the doing of A itself, and A is what the agent intended to do.

It is in this sense of "purposive" that each act in the moral field is purposive.

Some may find it strange that certain trivial acts turn out to be in the moral field. For example, putting on my left shoe in the morning is both a voluntary and purposive act, thus it is in the moral field. So is swallowing a bite of toast or opening the car door. These acts are usually trivial, yet they still have a moral property—they each are morally permissible (in virtually every instance of their occurrence). It turns out that the number of voluntary and purposive act-tokens that an average person is the agent of in one day runs into the thousands, and almost all of them are morally permissible. Even a serial murderer does hundreds of trivial acts each day that are morally permissible. Being insignificant is not a disqualifier for being in the moral field. Imagine someone asking childishly whether it is morally permissible to put on his own left shoe first or swallow his toast. Is not the truthful answer going to be, "Of course, it is morally permissible for you to do so"?

Nevertheless, the more interesting acts in the moral field are the ones that have some significant effects on the agent or on others. And the measure of a person's moral goodness or badness is not based on the number of morally permissible acts she does; it is based on the number and quality of the morally obligatory acts she does (or does not do) and the number and quality of impermissible acts she does.

Conclusion

The purpose of this chapter was to identify the moral field. I have made the case that it comprises all voluntary and purposive act-tokens, persons, and those states of affair that are, roughly speaking, the effects of human acts and are directly related to human well-being. I have also tried to show how a moral theory that is about act-tokens has implications for the morality of both persons and states of affairs, and that a moral theory about persons and/or states of affairs has implications for act-tokens. Thus moral theory can have either act-tokens or persons or states of affairs as its moral field and be a true moral theory with a complete moral field.

6

Moral Epistemology

One of the most difficult and controversial topics in metaethics is moral epistemology. Skepticism about our ability to have sufficient warrant for any moral convictions is one of the prevailing factors for the dominance of postmodern moral antirealism. The main question of moral epistemology can be asked in a variety of ways: how can we determine which moral judgments, moral precepts, and moral principles are true and which are false? How do we know which moral properties things in the moral field have? How do we know what the moral order is? Versions of these questions have engaged philosophers for millennia.

Of the two different kinds of moralists—moral realists and moral antirealists—moral realists are the only ones who have to struggle to find firm epistemological footing for moral judgments. Moral antirealists don't have the same problem because for a person to know a proposition, one necessary condition is that the proposition is true. As explained in chapter 1, expressivism, one main version of moral antirealism, is noncognitivist—a view on which moral utterances are neither true nor false. How could they have a truth value given that on this view there is no moral reality?[1] Moral constructivism, the other main version of moral antirealism, denies the existence of the moral order and advances only social morality,[2] and as such

---

1. The epistemological difficulty moral antirealists face making their case for what moral utterances are doing—moral hermeneutics—since on their account such language cannot be factual. This was explained in chapter 2.

2. As explained in chapter 1, "social morality" as I use it, refers only to the social mores of a society.

it does not have great difficulty with epistemological issues either. Social morality is concerned only with conduct that is accepted and approved in a particular society.[3] The epistemological basis for claims regarding social morality in society B are settled by examining what practices and conduct are accepted and approved in B. This is done by observing the people who are in B, by asking them what practices they approve, and by undertaking other empirical techniques. Social morality involves describing a contingent social reality, and as such it is a proper subject for sociologists rather than philosophers.

Moral epistemology is a subspecies of epistemology, and it will be important to take a quick look at one helpful line of development in philosophical epistemology in order to develop a moral epistemology. My intent is to give a clear and reasonable account of why it is that human beings can and do know many particular moral judgments and moral precepts—all sorts of moral propositions. My analysis begins by a consideration of how we can make normative *aesthetic* judgments. Like normative *moral* judgments, aesthetic judgments involve understanding how something measures up against a norm.

Aesthetic Judgment

As I recall it, thirty or forty years ago an American actor, Vincent Price, was on *The Tonight Show* with Johnny Carson. Price had a reputation for having a fine eye for oil paintings (as well as a developed appreciation for fine wine). Carson was doubtful of the enormous variation in the valuation of original oil paintings and, as I remember it, he thought it might be a sort of rigged art dealer gambit. So he had Price evaluate several oil paintings that he had never seen before. To the untrained eye, there was no great difference in the appearance of the paintings, yet their prices differed by thousands of dollars.[4] Price eyed the first painting, he said something like, "This is not very good; its value is only a few hundred dollars." The price tag attached to the back of the painting, out of Price's view, confirmed his

---

3. Any social morality in many respects will be consistent with the moral order, and so possibly be evidence of its content. The difficulty is that if one does not know in advance what the moral order is, one won't know in which respects a social morality is consistent with it.

4. The actual details of the account are my fabrication as I don't remember exactly what was said or how many paintings there were. The substance of the narrative is accurate.

estimate. Price moved on to the second painting, which he said was a very fine painting worth some thousands of dollars. Again his judgment was confirmed. Overall, in looking at four or five paintings, Price's estimate of their value was within 10% of the price assigned in the art gallery from which they had been borrowed.

It was clear from Price's comments that the judgment of artistic merit was almost an immediate response on his first viewing of a painting. Price did not analyze in detail the brush strokes, or colors, or shading, or perspective—rather, in one glance all was taken in sufficiently to warrant a judgment of value. When asked afterward making his assessment what accounted for the estimate made, Price would refer to the perspective and shading and the like, but the estimate was not a deduction from individual judgments regarding these features. Price did not first analyze the painting and then come to his judgment, it was almost instantaneous. If one had asked him how he could do this, he would have said that it was from a long history of viewing and evaluating oil paintings.

The same sort of normative aesthetic judgments take place all the time. People with a developed taste for wine can distinguish a fine wine from an inferior one with one brief swirl, sniff and taste. Again, the judgment is almost immediate, and the analysis follows along with the unique descriptive language wine connoisseurs use like "angular, dusty, gunpowdery, flabby, and jammy." People who have developed olfactory sensitivities and experience with perfumes can identify the better and the poorer varieties with a brief whiff. In a similar way, a professor with grading experience can read a student paper and give it a grade before writing down, or even consciously thinking of, its strengths and weaknesses. A basketball coach can watch a walk-on in a tryout for a few minutes and accurately size up his playing potential. I once asked a golf instructor how many swings he would need to see a golfer take in order to make a good estimate of his handicap, and he replied that he could almost do it by looking merely at how the golfer addressed the ball. The point is that people who have considerable experience, especially if they started quite young, often acquire the ability to make normative judgments about those things with which they are very familiar. In your own case, it is probable that you are able to quickly come to some judgments about practices with which you have some level of expertise. Perhaps you can effortlessly and quickly identify a good musician, a good engine design, or a good recipe. When people with such skills compare their evaluations, in many cases they will agree, even when those with less experience have strongly held contrary views. From the examples given it should be clear already that not everybody has the same level of expertise in making normative judgments—different people have different areas of expertise. Some people may be expert in a few areas, others may be expert in a dozen, and perhaps there are some who are not expert in any area at all.

Now what are we to make of this ability to make normative judgments that persons acquire? Should we adopt the view that those who demonstrate the expertise, say, in evaluating fine wines, are just guessing? Should we come to the view that their evaluation is no better than the judgments of those without any expertise? Should we conclude that any expertise is nothing more than a reflection of a particular culture—that fine wine in England may rate poorly in China, or that a great painting in Russia may be worthless in Argentina? Of course, culture is a factor in aesthetic evaluations, and what is truly beautiful may not be appreciated equally in every culture. Not every place is exposed to the same range of fine art or good products. But a fine wine is a fine wine even when in a culture where no one has the expertise to appreciate it properly. The judgment of a golf instructor can be tested against the scores the golfer shoots, so in this case (and many others) the judgments made can be objectively tested. If a person grew up listening only to country music, she could probably tell a good country song from a lousy one. She may not be able to appreciate Bach or Haydn. Yet Mozart's Symphony No. 40 is great music, even in a place where all that has been heard is country music. Consider the athlete who excels in cricket. Experts in cricket in England recognize and appreciate his skill, but few if any in the United States will have the same evaluation. They don't know what to look for—they haven't acquired the skill for evaluating cricket players. That doesn't mean that when this player is in the United States he is not an excellent cricket player. It's only that his particular athletic ability is not appreciated there. Similarly, a great painting by van Gogh is a great painting even in a culture which has experienced only cave paintings. The goodness that experts can perceive is an objective value, not a personal or social construct. That is why one can recognize their own deficiencies as well. I know that the 1982 Chateau Lafleur Pomerol is a wonderful wine,[5] but it

---

5. I would not know this had I not looked it up online and trusted the expertise of the sources.

would be wasted on me because I lack the experience and palate needed to truly appreciate it.

Vincent Price, and others with expertise, are generally able to articulate reasons for their immediate evaluative response to a work of art. But the response precedes the reasons, because the response is not a purely cognitive act—it includes an emotional reaction. Yet the reaction isn't irrational, and there are good reasons why an expert makes the normative judgments that she does.[6] The reasons an expert can react as she does is due to the fact that what is evaluated has objective value.

C. S. Lewis

C. S. Lewis makes similar points in an enlightening passage in *The Abolition of Man*. Lewis writes about different kinds of normative judgments, including both aesthetic and moral. It is so good, clear, and helpful that I quote it at length:

> Until quite modern times all teachers and even all men believed the universe to be such that certain emotional reactions on our part could be either congruous or incongruous to it—believed, in fact, that objects did not merely receive, but could *merit*, our approval or disapproval, our reverence, or our contempt. 'Can you be righteous,' asks Traherne, 'unless you be just in rendering to things their due esteem? All things were made to be yours and you were made to prize them according to their value.' St. Augustine defines virtue as *ordo amoris*, the ordinate condition of the affections in which every object is accorded that kind and degree of love which is appropriate to it. Aristotle says that the aim of education is to make the pupil like and dislike what he ought. When the age for reflective thought comes, the pupil who has been thus trained in 'ordinate affections' or 'just sentiments' will easily find the first principles in Ethics: but to the corrupt man they will never be visible at all and he can make no progress in that science. Plato before him has said the same. The little human animal will not at first have the right responses. It must be trained to feel pleasure, liking, disgust, and hatred at those things which really are pleasant, likeable, disgusting, and hateful. In the *Republic*, the well-nurtured

---

6. I do not doubt that it is possible that a person could have expert-like reactions to a work of art without knowing or being able to articulate reasons for his reaction. But this would be exceptional. The kind of expertise that allows for excellence at making normative judgments often has a cognitive component, but it need not always.

> youth is one 'who would see most clearly whatever was amiss in ill-made works of man or ill-grown works of nature, and with a just distaste would blame and hate the ugly even from his earliest years and would give delighted praise to beauty, receiving it into his soul and being nourished by it, so that he becomes a man of gentle heart. All this before he is of an age to reason; so that when Reason at length comes to him, then, bred as he has been, he will hold out his hands in welcome and recognize her because of the affinity he bears to her.'[7]

Part of Lewis's summation has to do with when and how a person can acquire the proper sentiments to become one who recognizes objective value. My argument thus far has merely been to illustrate that human beings have the capacity for such sentiments, and that these sentiments are based in the objective value of what is evaluated. It is an interesting and perdurable idea in the Western classical tradition that the training of our sentiments is best when it is started at an early age. On this point both Plato and Aristotle agree.

Lewis goes on to speak about the objective standard of value that is at the heart of the classical view:

> This conception in all its forms, Platonic, Aristotelian, Stoic, Christian, and Oriental alike, I shall henceforth refer to for brevity simply as 'the *Tao*'. Some of the accounts of it which I have quoted will seem, perhaps, to many of you merely quaint or even magical. But what is common to them all is something we cannot neglect. It is the doctrine of objective value, the belief that certain attitudes are really true, and others really false, to the kind of thing the universe is and the kind of things we are. Those who

---

7. Lewis, *Abolition of Man*, 25–27. Lewis goes on to cite eastern and mid-eastern sources: "In early Hinduism that conduct in men which can be called good consists in conformity to, or almost participation in, the *Rta*—that great ritual or pattern of nature and supernature which is revealed alike in the cosmic order, the moral virtues, and the ceremonial of the temple. Righteousness, correctness, order, the *Rta*, is constantly identified with *satya* or truth, correspondence to reality. As Plato said that the Good was 'beyond existence' and Wordsworth that through virtue the stars were strong, so the Indian masters say that the gods themselves are born of the *Rta* and obey it. The Chinese also speak of a great thing (the greatest thing) called the *Tao*. It is the reality beyond all predicates, the abyss that was before the Creator Himself. It is Nature, it is the Way, the Road. It is the Way in which the universe goes on, the Way in which things everlastingly emerge, stilly and tranquilly, into space and time. It is also the Way which every man should tread in imitation of that cosmic and supercosmic progression, conforming all activities to that great exemplar. 'In ritual,' say the Analects, 'it is harmony with Nature that is prized.' The ancient Jews likewise praise the Law as being 'true.'

Moral Epistemology

know the *Tao* can hold that to call children delightful or old men venerable is not simply to record a psychological fact about our own parental or filial emotions at the moment, but to recognize a quality which *demands* a certain response from us whether we make it or not. I myself do not enjoy the society of small children: because I speak from within the *Tao* I recognize this as a defect in myself—just as a man may have to recognize that he is tone deaf or colour blind. And because our approvals and disapprovals are thus recognitions of objective value or responses to an objective order, therefore emotional states can be in harmony with reason (when we feel liking for what ought to be approved) or out of harmony with reason (when we perceive that liking is due but cannot feel it). No emotion is, in itself, a judgment: in that sense all emotions and sentiments are alogical. But they can be reasonable or unreasonable as they conform to Reason or fail to conform. The heart never takes the place of the head: but it can, and should, obey it.[8]

Lewis adduces evidence from many traditions to write about objective value and the ability people can have to recognize it. He blends aesthetic and moral values together because they are ontologically and epistemologically similar. With respect to recognizing objective *moral* value, Lewis says that it is an acquired skill a person needs to start learning from an early age. Only then will one's emotions be "in harmony with reason." Lewis also notes that one can know that something is good or beautiful but lack appreciation for it. He attributes this to underdeveloped or badly developed emotions. In his own case, he knows he should enjoy the company of small children but in fact he does not. This he takes as a personal defect like being color blind.[9] In a similar way, I recognize that delight is the fitting reaction to a glass of 1982 Chateau Lafleur Pomerol, but it would not be my reaction.

This raises the question of how one can know that something is good or beautiful if one's emotions are not properly trained to respond correctly. Lewis does not address this question directly, but when a person has some of his emotions properly trained to perceive a variety of aesthetic and moral values, he will be able to understand that there are some gaps in his emotional training with the result that in some areas his responses are not always in harmony with reason. In such cases one can know something is

---

8. Ibid., 28–30.

9. I don't think this is the best analogy, as color blindness is not a product of poor training. A better illustration may be the inability to, say, ride a unicycle (although this analogy also breaks down in two ways: learning to ride a unicycle is of doubtful value and it could be learned later in life).

good or beautiful by the reliable witness of those who have the appropriate reaction and can give reasons why. With respect to one's acts, it would be wonderful to have been so trained as to truly enjoy doing what one is morally obliged to do and to hate what is morally impermissible. The sad truth is that while one can have many fitting reactions to event act-tokens, past, present and future, for every person there are event act-tokens that ought to be done and are not enjoyed, and some that ought not to be done and are enjoyed.

Providing examples of people who are expert in making normative aesthetic and moral judgments, and showing how it is an ability recognized in many great cultural traditions, is not the same thing as giving a philosophical account of how moral judgments are known. Such an account would be critically important in providing a means by which we can have some confidence that a moral judgment is true. So now we move from a description of human capacity to recognize objective moral values to a philosophical explanation of it. We start by considering epistemology generally.

Moral Evidentialism

Philosophical epistemology arises in part because most philosophers agree that a person has an intellectual obligation not to believe foolishness. This obligation may be a moral obligation, although sometimes it is cited as an intellectual duty. W. K. Clifford explains this obligation in plain terms: "it is wrong always, everywhere, and for anyone to believe anything upon insufficient evidence."[10] Other versions of this duty are more nuanced, for example, some have said that the strength of believing something ought to be in direct proportion to the evidence one has for it. We can call this "the evidence obligation." A variety of this obligation can be found in John Locke, David Hume, Bertrand Russell, Anthony Flew, Michael Scriven, and many others. What kind of obligation is this? If to believe something, or to keep believing something, or to not believe something, is a voluntary and purposive act, then each instance of it is either morally permissible or impermissible.[11] In contrast, Alvin Plantinga concludes that what we believe is

---

10. Clifford, *Ethics*, 295.

11. Cf. chapter 5 where the question of which acts are moral (as opposed to amoral) is addressed directly.

usually not under our direct control, so he thinks that notions of duty and obligation don't apply to the formation and sustaining of what we believe.[12]

The evidence obligation is the basis for classical foundationalism (CF). CF is a view about which beliefs adequately meet the evidence obligation. According to CF there are two kinds of beliefs that can meet this obligation, *properly basic ones* and *non-basic ones*. Properly basic beliefs are beliefs that are either self-evident, incorrigible,[13] or evident to the senses—all matters about which we are unlikely to be mistaken. In order for a non-basic belief to meet the evidence obligation it must be held in proportion to the evidence provided for it by properly basic beliefs. CF has a long history and a lot of initial appeal as it seems to give reasonable conditions for regulating beliefs.

The initial appeal of CF, however, is misleading; on closer consideration it turns out that it cannot be correct. Not only is it false—it is self-referentially incoherent. That it is false can be seen from a one example. My belief *that I ate toast this morning* does not meet any of the three conditions for being a basic belief: it is not a self-evident proposition, it is not incorrigible for me (I could be confusing yesterday's breakfast with today's), and it is not evident to my senses (I cannot see or hear or taste or smell or touch my toast now). It is a memory, and memories are regularly mistaken. Nor is it a proposition that is evidenced by any properly basic beliefs I do have. Thus according to CF I have an obligation not to believe it—believing it violates an intellectual duty I have. But this is clearly a mistake. It is obviously permissible for me to believe that I ate toast for breakfast this morning. So the conditions for what a person is permitted to believe are too restricted by CF. And the problem with CF is even deeper; it is self-referentially incoherent. The claim *one should only believe what is either properly basic or evidenced by what is properly basic* is itself neither properly basic nor evidenced by what is properly basic. So according to the theory, the theory itself ought not be believed.

Warrant for Moral Knowledge

Classical foundationalism had a long run in Western philosophy. Now that its dominance has ended, a variety of epistemological theories have surfaced to replace it. No philosopher has written more clearly or with more insight

---

12. Plantinga, *Proper Function*, vii.

13. To be "incorrigible" means that the knower who believes it cannot be mistaken, for example, "I seem to be experiencing pain in my left foot."

on issues in philosophical epistemology than Alvin Plantinga. While his overarching purpose is to address epistemological issues regarding theistic belief, he deals carefully with many of the issues in philosophical epistemology. What I will say about moral epistemology has been in large part informed by his trilogy, *Warrant: the Current Debate, Warrant and Proper Function*, and *Warranted Christian Belief*.[14] The common notion in each title of these three books is "warrant(ed)." But what is warrant? And how is it connected to knowledge?

Traditionally, for a proposition *p* to be known by person A, it needed to meet three conditions: A believes p, A is justified in believing p (A has evidence for p), and p is true. Of these three conditions, the first and the third seem indisputable. A person cannot be said to know something she does not believe; even though sometimes in speaking casually we might say something like, "I know that our team won, but I can't believe it." Nor can a person know something that is not true. You cannot know that the earth is flat or that the Chicago Cubs won the World Series in 2014. So the focus in philosophical epistemology has been on the second condition: that A has evidence for p. As we have seen in the case of CF, the idea of being justified because of "having evidence" is not clear, so the new terminology for the second condition is *A has warrant for p*. "Warrant for p" is that which a person needs, in addition to true belief, in order to have knowledge.

This explains the role of warrant, but it does not explain how one gets or achieves it. For that we turn to Plantinga's explanation of warrant. After a thorough consideration of alternative proposals for what constitutes warrant, Plantinga finds that all of them have defects. Plantinga then submits an account of warrant that he cogently explains and meticulously defends. He determines that "A belief has warrant if and only if it is produced by cognitive faculties functioning properly in a congenial epistemic environment according to a design plan aimed at the production of true belief."[15] Warrant for a belief is not a property of what the belief is, rather it is connected to how it comes to be believed. If we substitute "moral belief" for "belief" we get:

---

14. My extension of Plantinga's epistemology to moral knowledge is piecemeal (and may even fail to follow his theory exactly); there is little doubt that what I say raises all kinds of philosophical questions. I can do no better than to recommend to the reader to take up Plantinga himself for an enjoyable and yet rigorous consideration of many issues that are outside the scope of this chapter.

15. Plantinga, *Christian Belief*, 498.

Moral Epistemology

A moral belief has warrant if and only if it is produced by cognitive faculties functioning properly in a congenial epistemic environment according to a design plan aimed at the production of true moral belief.

There are three parts of this explanation of warrant on which I will elaborate and explain in connection with the warrant for moral beliefs:

(1) produced by cognitive faculties functioning properly

(2) in a congenial epistemic environment

(3) according to a design plan aimed at the production of true belief.[16]

Produced by Cognitive Faculties Functioning Properly

In order for a belief to have warrant, it must be formed and sustained by a person's cognitive faculties functioning properly. This does not need a great deal of explanation, because it is obvious that beliefs are formed and sustained in a person's mind by the functioning of mental abilities, i.e. cognitive faculties. I believe that I ate a piece of toast for breakfast this morning because I remember doing so, my memory has stored this belief and I am able to recall it. My memory is functioning properly, because what I remember actually happened. If my memory is not functioning properly, I may forget things that a properly functioning memory would recall, or perhaps I may remember things that never happened.

A person's memory, like other epistemic faculties, is one that can function well or poorly. A person can even have a good memory for some things and a poor one for other things. I have trouble remembering people's names, but I remember historical dates easily. To say a cognitive faculty is functioning properly does not mean it functions perfectly. Memories can be better or worse, and the warrant of the beliefs they produce is a matter of degree. The warrant I have for the belief that my wife's birthday is in July is greater than the warrant for my belief that the person I met yesterday was Sam. Warrant comes in degrees. A person's memory may be abnormally poor, so that it often malfunctions. A person may think she remembers things that have not happened, or one could forget things that happened moments ago. Elderly people sometimes experience extreme memory

---

16. My purpose is not to argue for or defend Plantinga's conception of warrant, for that you can read Plantinga's engaging and persuasive argument about it, which I highly recommend. See Plantinga, *Proper Function*, 3–47.

malfunction, and such losses are very difficult. In such cases their memories have little warrant. A faculty that is involved in producing a belief is functioning properly when it is not suffering from a malfunction, when it is functioning as it ought to. It is difficult to state exactly the conditions that need to be met for something to be functioning properly. A human heart that beats irregularly, a car engine that will not start, or a bird with a broken wing—are all examples of something not functioning properly. If we did not have a sense of proper function, we would not know what needs to be adjusted, corrected, or fixed. If we did not know what a properly functioning memory is, we would not notice when someone's memory is failing.

Plantinga deals with a wide range of beliefs: memory beliefs,[17] perceptual beliefs,[18] *a priori* beliefs,[19] inductive beliefs,[20] and others. He does not, however, consider aesthetic or moral beliefs.[21] His analysis of how beliefs have warrant can be extended to moral beliefs, that is, to beliefs about what is morally permissible and what is morally impermissible. The cognitive faculty primarily responsible for producing and sustaining moral beliefs is the *conscience*.[22] As the memory is the faculty that produces recollections of the past, so the conscience is the faculty that produces moral beliefs. The conscience, when presented with an act done by an agent, whether a past, present, or future possibility, forms a belief as to the moral properties of the act. When things are going properly, this response is unmediated. It is not a belief that is based on other beliefs; it is basic. When the conscience functions properly, the beliefs it produces are unmediated responses in accord with reason but are not the results of reasoning. Like the judgments that are made when a wine critic evaluates a wine, the moral judgments of a properly functioning conscience precede the rational analysis that lies behind and contributes to the judgment. What typically triggers the con-

---

17. Plantinga, *Proper Function*, 57–64.
18. Ibid., 89–101.
19. Ibid., 102–21.
20. Ibid., 122–36.

21. Ibid., 48. Plantinga makes the point that his epistemic coverage is incomplete, both because he doesn't discuss all the "main modules of our epistemic establishment" (including the moral and aesthetic) and because his discussion of the other modules are primarily aimed at elucidating the idea of warrant.

22. Being able to name or individuate the human faculties that are instrumental in producing beliefs is not a required exercise in Plantinga's epistemology. It is noteworthy, however, that moral beliefs have been considered important enough to have their primary producer named.

science to produce beliefs is when it is presented by an act that is of some importance because of its possible effects. Yet if a person with a properly functioning conscience is asked about an act with relatively trivial effects, the conscience can help to discern the moral property the act has or, if a future act, would have. After a pick pocket lifts your wallet, your properly functioning conscience immediately forms the belief that it is morally permitted for you to chase after him but morally impermissible to take out a gun and shoot him.

As in the case of other critical skills, some people have a more highly developed conscience than others. Just as a music critic can easily discern the difference between two performances of Beethoven's fifth symphony, a person with a well-developed conscience can discern moral differences between two similar acts performed by different agents. Like the wine critic who can easily recognize an inferior year, a person with a developed conscience can recognize an act that is morally impermissible from a similar act that is morally permissible. The conscience is a faculty that is not equally developed in every person, so disagreements may arise. But, of course, disagreement does not mean there is no truth. In the same way that some people can see more clearly than others, and some can taste with more discrimination, and others can hear with perfect pitch, so some people have a conscience which gives them a superior ability to identify the moral properties of act-tokens.

The conscience can be corrupted, and as a result fail to function properly. If a young child is raised in an environment where shoplifting is not only condoned but praised, likely the conscience will be malformed about acts of shoplifting, and perhaps it will be corrupted about stealing in general. If a child grows up in a sexually abusive environment, his conscience about sexual acts may be less reliable and may be very dysfunctional. But it does not require bad experiences to corrupt a conscience; some people seem to be born without a properly functioning conscience, perhaps similar to how a person is born deaf or without a sense of taste. Lacking a properly functioning conscience makes persons a danger to themselves and others, as they have no internal mechanism that helps them to distinguish between right and wrong and set moral boundaries on what they should do.

To a great extent the ability to form warranted moral beliefs seems to depend on how a person has been raised, and what sort of moral training she has received. Later in life it is much more difficult to acquire the proper emotional reactions. One can learn some of the properties that typically tend to make an act permissible or impermissible late in life, but without proper early training this learning usually is insufficient to produce the appropriate sentiments when confronted with an important act. While the functioning of a person's conscience seldom improves to any degree in adulthood, it can become selectively dysfunctional. The first time Martha took an illegal drug she knew it was morally wrong, but she did it anyway. The second time her conscience was a bit quieter, and by the time it had become a routine her conscience was silent on the issue—she did not recognize that it was wrong anymore. And what is true for Martha and drug use seems to affect any person who routinely violates his or her conscience. Eventually the conscience loses its ability to discern moral truth regarding those acts that it originally deemed morally impermissible. This can happen to individuals, and it can also happen to communities and even societies. Evil can develop in society when enough consciences have lost their function with respect to some area of life and duty; this is what seems to have happened to the Nazis in their treatment of Jews and other minorities. A climate of social opinion can develop in which consciences cease to function properly in some area of life and great social evils are tolerated—even celebrated.

These ideas as to the factors and occasions in which a person acquires a properly functioning conscience and one of the ways a conscience can be corrupted are not part of the central claim of this chapter. The claim to focus on here is that the conscience is a cognitive faculty which, when functioning properly, forms and sustains moral beliefs which have warrant, unless the environment in which the beliefs are formed is not epistemically congenial for the formation of such beliefs.

A Congenial Epistemic Environment

A person in a darkened room is not in a congenial epistemic environment for the formation of perceptual beliefs. A person in a space filled with holograms and mirrors is not in a congenial environment for the formation of true perceptual beliefs. A person's cognitive faculties for the formation of beliefs can be functioning properly, but if the environment is not congenial to the formation of beliefs, the beliefs that will be formed will lack warrant.

What is a congenial epistemic environment in which a properly functioning conscience works to give a person a warranted moral belief? If

Moral Epistemology

someone reports an act, but omits salient details, a person with a properly functioning conscience may come to a moral judgment about the act that is in error. A person needs to be aware of all the relevant facts about an act, including its context, the agent's intentions, and the foreseeable consequences in order to form a moral belief that has warrant. If you only know that Sam deceived Bob, but you don't know that Sam's deceit was in order to preserve the surprise of a birthday party for Bob, you don't know enough to make a moral judgment that is warranted. This is where the adage about not jumping to conclusions is the best policy. Earlier we claimed that experts can make normative judgments quickly because such judgments are more like emotional responses than rational calculations. But an expert in oil painting needs to see the whole painting, and not just one corner of it. A music critic needs to hear more than the opening chord to make a sound judgment about a set performed by a band. A wine expert swirls, sniffs, imbibes and sloshes before forming a final judgment about a vintage. So a person needs to be aware of the salient details of what is being judged in order to form a moral belief that will have warrant.

There are other environments one can imagine in which the conscience will not produce a warranted moral belief. Jack is taking a walk in the woods, when he comes into a clearing and sees two men stealthily approaching and then viciously attacking a third man who is sleeping next to a cold campfire. Jack sees this attack as morally wrong and so tries to think of a way of assisting the person under attack. What Jack doesn't know is that the men he sees are all actors rehearsing a scene in a movie that will be filmed later that day. His intervention is neither needed nor wanted. This is a case where Jack lacks some of the salient information that is needed, but it is not because of anyone's intentional deception of Jack. Jack did not receive a partial report, nor did he only see part of the event act-token. He was there and he saw the whole thing, but he didn't understand the context.

Still other sorts of inadequate epistemic environments for the conscience to form warranted beliefs can be imagined. A person could mistake an automaton for a human person, or a computer program for a real therapist.[23] A witness could completely misconstrue what act-token or event act-token an agent is attempting, and doing something other than what is intended is also relevant information for a moral evaluation. If Tom is trying to murder Henry by shooting him, but is such a bad shot he misses Henry

---

23. Some people have thought Eliza, a computer program that emulates a Rogerian therapist, is a real person.

and inadvertently shoots Ralph, who himself is trying to stab Henry, it may seem that Tom is morally praiseworthy. Knowing that Tom was trying to murder Henry is relevant to a moral evaluation of what he did. Foreseeable consequences are also part of the environment of an act, and may not be congenial for the conscience to form the correct judgment. Imagine a possible world in which natural physical laws are sufficiently altered so that smacking someone with a two-by-four causes no pain, no damage, and is an accepted way to display affection. A conscience trained in the actual world would need some significant readjustment to function properly in that environment, since in the actual world such conduct would cause injury. Anticipating the foreseeable causal consequences of an act are part of the epistemic environment.[24] In order for a properly functioning conscience to form warranted moral beliefs, a person needs to have sufficient information about the context, agent, and foreseeable consequences of the event act-token. When these conditions are met, the epistemic environment is congenial to the formation of warranted moral beliefs.

According to a Design Plan Aimed at the Production of True Belief

A human organ, say a kidney, has a specific function in the biological life of a person. When a person's kidneys are functioning properly, they accomplish for the human organism what they are designed to do. "Designed" in this context does not mean that a design plan is something done by a conscious intelligence. Design is simply the best word to describe something's structure which allows it to serve in the role or purpose it plays. Here a theist may claim that God has designed organisms to function as they do, perhaps using evolutionary processes, but Plantinga avers this is not required to grasp the relevant idea of a design plan.[25] Plantinga's use of the idea of a "design plan" is carefully delineated, making use of several key distinctions. First, a snapshot design plan describes how something is supposed to work at a specific time; the master design plan includes the expected changes that are expected to take place over time. So a small child's faculty of speech is

---

24. Facts about the pretext, context, agent intention, and foreseeable consequences of an event act-token are relevant but do not determine the moral property of the act. In a similar way the perspective, lighting, subject matter, etc. are relevant to the artistic merit of a painting but do not determine it. Some say that such facts "supervene" on judgments, which is fine with me, but such facts do not imply the judgment.

25. Plantinga cites atheist Daniel Dennett as speaking of an organism's design and of evolution as producing it in Plantinga, *Proper Function*, 13.

working according to the master design plan when a six month old cannot say any words. If the child still cannot speak at three years of age, his speech faculty is not functioning according to the design plan. A design plan also includes how something will function in unusual conditions. If Teresa is severely dehydrated, her kidneys will respond in a predictable way, and in so doing will be following their design plan. A design plan does not include all possible unusual circumstances; if natural laws were to be altered or if there were an extensive change to something's structure, its design plan may not account for what to expect in such changed circumstances.

A person's conscience can be developed in circumstances that are detrimental to its functionality. If a person is raised in an abusive family, he may never develop a conscience that is able to recognize the moral properties of abusive acts. As some people are tone deaf, and some are color blind, a person can have a conscience that is dysfunctional regarding a whole range of act-types. As a blind person cannot judge visual arts, and a deaf person cannot evaluate music performances, so a person can have a totally dysfunctional conscience and not be able to discern the difference between right and wrong. In severe cases, a person's conscience may be thoroughly corrupted, yet even this is no reason to think that the conscience is never a reliable epistemic faculty.

The main challenge to identifying the conscience as the primary faculty for moral discernment is the claim that the conscience is engineered by evolution as a faculty to restrain persons from anti-social behavior. From this perspective the purpose of the conscience is not to help the individual find the truth about how one should act, rather it is to help society protect itself from unbridled self interest. The evolutionary design plan is not aimed at truth, but at social preservation. So on the evolutionary view the conscience does not meet one condition for warranted moral belief—that it be a cognitive faculty aimed at true belief.

This view of the conscience makes you wonder how the selfish little human animal came to accept the dictates of his conscience, especially as it tended to cut into his self-interest. The evidence that any other species shows the effects of a conscience is negligible. Male lions show no compunction about killing the offspring of another male when they take over a pride. You would think survival of the species would have helped lions to learn that it was in the interest of their species to let lion cubs live. But lions are not interested in the survival of their society, except to the extent it directly benefits them for hunting, fighting, and reproducing.

An alternative explanation for the purpose of the conscience is that it is an emotional warning system. When a person is about to do something that may have a negative outcome, the conscience gives a warning against such a course of action. This would have survival benefits, even if there are occasional cases where the alarm goes off incorrectly. The purpose of an alarm is not to always be accurate about the danger—overestimating it occasionally is acceptable, as long as it always gives warning about real dangers. So it is not part of a design plan aimed at truth, but rather is aimed at survival.

This explanation of the purpose of the conscience will not do. First, the conscience does not always produce moral beliefs that align with a person taking the safest possible course of action. If all we know about a person's choice of action is that it was motivated solely out of concern that it may be dangerous for the agent, we have insufficient evidence for making a moral judgment. If the purpose of the conscience was to steer one clear of danger, then making a choice to steer clear of danger would be morally obligatory. Yet we often recognize that those who put themselves in harm's way are doing something morally permissible and praiseworthy. The well-functioning conscience will often condemn acts that are self-preserving. Second, a person's conscience does not only apply to his or her own choices. We make moral judgments about the acts that others do. We make moral judgments about acts that have been done in the past. As we have seen,[26] a person's ability to make moral judgments is not limited to his own acts and it extends to acts that were done in the past. On the explanation suggested, however, these functions would have no part in the design plan of the conscience—to warn the individual of potential dangers.

The most viable explanation for the design plan of the conscience is that it is to produce and maintain moral beliefs that are true. When a conscience does this, in a congenial epistemic environment, then our moral beliefs have warrant.

Conclusion

Following Plantinga's definition of warrant, I have argued that the conscience is the primary cognitive faculty for producing and maintaining

26. Cf. chapter 2.

moral beliefs. Because the conscience functions in accord with a design plan that is aimed at the production of true belief, when it is functioning properly in a congenial epistemic environment, the moral beliefs that it produces have warrant. In many cases, such beliefs have warrant and one not only believes but knows the moral truth.

7

Grounding the Moral Order

Our venture into metaethics cannot end without at least a brief consideration of one of the most debated topics in realist metaethics—the *grounding* of the moral order. The central question regarding grounding can be asked in several ways: why is the moral order as it is rather than something different? Why do moral agents have the moral obligations that they do and not different ones? These questions are not about *what* is morally permissible and what is not—the normative moral questions—they are about *why* something that is morally permissible is morally permissible or *why* something that is morally impermissible is morally impermissible.

Understanding the ground of the moral order is of great interest to moral philosophers. Part of the reason for this interest is philosophical curiosity regarding a disputed issue. On the normative level—the level of making moral judgments—moralists often agree on almost every moral question. But on the metaethical level they frequently disagree. So while all reasonable moralists agree that torturing small children is morally impermissible, yet they may disagree quite widely on *why* it is wrong. One group may think that the reason it is morally wrong to torture small children is that it is against God's command. Others may say that the reason it is morally wrong is because children deserve some protection as human beings. Still others may believe that it is irrational to torture small children. This disagreement is about what non-moral states of affairs ground the moral state of affairs.

Typically the issue of the grounding of the moral order is taken up by moral realists, not moral antirealists. The latter do not think there is a moral order. At most, antirealists think there are social moralities. The question of why one social morality is what it is, and not other than it is, has to do with the history and local conditions of the society that accepts and approves it. As I explained in chapter 1, that is a question for sociologists. Since moral antirealists do not think there is any moral order, it does not make sense for them to wonder why it is what it is.

In this chapter I will first try to explain more precisely what grounding the moral order means. Then we will consider different answers to the question, both secular and religious, as to what grounds the moral order. Finally, we will consider whether the question of the grounding of the moral order has one true answer.

Grounding

In Plato's dialogue *Euthyphro* the concept of grounding is introduced in a narrative context. Socrates meets Euthyphro, a man on his way to court to prosecute his father, a fact which strikes Socrates as unusual. Socrates comments that Euthyphro must have a well-developed concept of what the right thing to do is, that is, what is "pious" (Gk. *hoision*, occasionally *eusebia*), a term meaning to act in accord with divine law.[1] For the ancients, it was a given that the moral order was divine law, but it is not so for us.[2] Socrates then asks Euthyphro to explain his understanding of divine law (the moral order). At first Euthyphro gives Socrates some examples of morally right acts,[3] but Socrates presses him for a definition. Euthyphro then suggests that a morally right act is one that the gods love. Socrates points out that the gods disagree about some things, sometimes even about what a person should do. Then Socrates helps Euthyphro come to the definition that the morally right thing to do is what all the gods love. Socrates applauds this answer, and then asks: do the gods all love right acts because they are morally right, or are they morally right acts because the gods love them? After having the question explained to him, Euthyphro says that the gods love them because they are morally right. To which Socrates replies that if this is the case, then Euthyphro's definition is not helpful, because it does not

---

1. Plato, *Euthyphro* 4b.
2. As a result, it is fair to understand Socrates to be asking about what I have been calling the moral order.
3. Using "morally right" is ambiguous, as noted in chapter 3, but I use it here because it is not clear whether Plato intends "morally permissible" or "morally obligatory."

explain *why* an act is morally right.[4] If the gods love an act because it is morally right, then an act's being morally right is logically prior to its being loved by the gods. Euthyphro's answer to Socrates is sufficient to produce a moral system principle, since what he claims implies that *x is loved by all the gods* and *x is morally right* are logically coextensive. I'll come back to this below. The point to note here is that, as a philosopher, Socrates is not interested in what property is coextensive with *being morally right*—he is interested in that property by which what is morally permissible and what is morally impermissible can be distinguished. He is interested in *why* any act is morally right. Socrates wants to know what brings about or metacauses the moral order—or what grounds the moral order.

The questions of why something is and why it is the way it is are questions whose answers begin with "because," a word derived from the middle English "by cause." A child asks, "Why does it rain?" and a parent says something like, "Because clouds are made of water." "Why" questions regarding events or states of affairs are questions about causation. One can ask "why" questions about physical events like rain, or about the existence or nature of something: "Why are there trees?" or "Why is Sam so tall?" or "Why is it cold in the winter?" Of course, many events are the result of a sequence of events that cause it. The cue ball strikes the eight-ball, which strikes the five-ball, which hits the nine-ball, which goes in the pocket. If someone asks, "Why did the nine-ball go in the pocket?" there are multiple causes and a full answer would include all of them. The short answer would be that the five-ball struck it causing it to roll into the pocket. We can distinguish between the *first cause* and the *secondary causes*. The first cause in the account is the motion of the cue ball. Each succeeding event is caused by a prior event, and the sequencing is important for a correct understanding of what happened. The eight-ball striking the five-ball and the five-ball striking the nine-ball are secondary causes of the nine-ball being pocketed. One event, the first cause, starts the ball rolling, so to speak, and all the succeeding causes are secondary. All the causes of an event that are not its primary cause are secondary causes. The last cause in a causal chain, the cause just preceding the event or state of affairs, can be considered *the most proximate secondary cause*. In the present case the five-ball striking

---

4. Remember that in chapter 4 we noted that it is the non-moral property that metacauses the moral property. Euthyphro gets this backwards, and gives an explanation of why the gods love an act rather than how an act comes to be morally right.

the nine-ball is the most proximate secondary cause of the nine-ball's being pocketed.

In the case of something metaphysical like the moral order, physical causation will not do, so we need something like "metacausality," a concept which was introduced in chapter 4 on moral principles.[5] I pointed out that there are at least two kinds of moral principles. One kind I called a *moral system principle*, which is a principle that links some non-moral property with some moral property, so that if something has one, it must have the other. This is the kind of principle Euthyphro's final answer to Socrates's inquiry could have generated. With such a principle the two propositions *something x has the non-moral property NM* and *x has the moral property MM* are logically equivalent, but the principle does not indicate that it is the non-moral state of affairs that brings about or causes the moral state of affairs. So while moral system principles generate a moral system, such principles fail what I call "the Euthyphro test"—giving an explanation of why something has the moral property it does. Thus there is a good reason for doubting that moralists usually intend their principles as merely moral system principles. Like Socrates, we don't just want simply to know how to distinguish what is morally permissible and morally impermissible; we want to know *why* something is MP or MI. We want to know the ground of the moral order, and we get that with an explanatory moral principle.

The second kind of moral principle which I explained in chapter 4 is an *explanatory moral principle*, in which part of the principle is that *x is NM metacauses x is MM*. Metacausality is an asymmetrical relationship which holds between two states of affairs such that the two states of affairs always occur together, yet one of the states of affairs brings about or "causes" the other. That is the asymmetry.[6] In explanatory moral principles, for example, one might propose a utilitarian principle, for example, *for any act x, and only for any act x, x results in as much net good as any other act available to the agent at the time metacauses that x is morally permissible.*[7]

---

5. It is defined as follows: For any two states of affairs, P and Q, P metacauses Q if and only if (1) P brings it about that Q (and not vice versa); and (2) the propositions corresponding to P and Q, viz. (x)Px and (x)Qx, are logical equivalents.

6. In metaphysics, and in most of philosophy, the issues are rarely about physical causation. Yet often the issues involve "why" questions, so something like metacausality is often needed.

7. On this view, it is also the case that if an act is morally permissible, then it has the property of being the act that results in more net good than any other available to the agent at the time, but the state of affairs expressed in the antecedent does not metacause

Here the non-moral state of affairs metacauses the moral state of affairs. Unlike physical causality where the events are temporally sequential, when one state of affairs metacauses another, neither one occurs temporally prior to the other. The two states of affairs always occur together, and in moral principles it is the non-moral state of affairs that brings about the moral state of affairs and not vice versa. So on this utilitarian view, the answer to the question "Why is act x morally permissible?" is that act x is metacaused by the state of affairs *x results in as much net good as any other available to the agent at the time.*

With this reminder about metacausality we can return to the question of grounding. For something A to ground something B, A brings about B or A metacauses B. This means that A is logically prior to B and A is the reason for B—it answers the question "why B?" We need to say more, however, about grounding, since, as in the cases of physical causation, it is possible for a state of affairs to have more proximate and less proximate secondary metacauses. (Recall that a sequence of metacauses is not a temporal sequence but a logical one.) So, for example, the state of affairs *p is actual* metacauses that *p is true* which in turn metacauses *p is not false*.[8]

Which of all the causes and metacauses in a chain is the ground? Are they all? Any of the metacauses or physical causes in a chain is part of the ground, but as one becomes more proximate, its relationship to the effect has more specific explanatory power. The child's question, "Why is it raining?" is generally answered by speaking about rain clouds. More remote causes may involve upper atmospheric winds, plunging air pressure or an approaching cold front. Religious parents may trace the primary cause of rain to God. For theists, "It is God's will" may be one answer to very many "why" questions.[9] But often there are multiple effects of remote secondary causes, making such remote causes less of an explanation for some specific occurrence. "It is God's will" is one explanation for almost everything, and as such not very helpful in understanding why one thing occurred rather than another. Upper atmospheric winds are instrumental in bringing about many more effects than rain, and so they do not provide a very helpful explanation of why it is raining. A more specific and helpful answer to

---

the state of affairs expressed in the consequent.

8. I suppose one could dispute whether p is true metacauses p is not false, although that seems like the right order to me.

9. Any non-physical causes are less proximate, except in the case of miracles or God's direct acting, and are properly bracketed out of scientific explanations. Thus it is *scientifically* unacceptable to attribute the rain to God, even if it is true.

the question of why it is raining identifies the more proximate secondary causes, perhaps something like the build-up of dark clouds. The most proximate secondary cause is what brings about the effect most directly, and thus is often the best short answer to why questions.

In the case of metaphysical questions as to the ground of something, a full answer would trace the metacauses of it back to the primary metacause; the best short answer is to identify the most proximate secondary metacause,[10] which is to give its *immediate ground*. But even more remote metacauses provide some explanation for why something is, and so are part of its ground. An explanatory moral principle involves a claim that some non-moral state of affairs is a metacause of some moral state of affairs, and as such it is identifying at least part of the ground of the moral order—although it may not be identifying the most proximate metacause.

The Ground of the Moral Order

Philosophers have sorted out into general categories the various kinds or types of non-moral states of affairs that moralists have identified in their moral principles. Two categories that are often distinguished are *naturalism* and *non-naturalism*. *Naturalism* is the name given to any view that grounds the moral order in a state of affairs that is empirically discernible, like *x produces pleasure*. *Non-naturalism* is the name given to any view which maintains that the non-moral state of affairs that grounds the moral order is not empirically discernible, like *x is the will of God*.[11] Another example of a non-naturalist moral theory, and one which does not involve theism, is *rationalist* moral theory. Such a theory holds that some logical property of an act or agent metacauses an act's moral property. For example, Alan Gewirth proposes such a view, making an interesting argument that moral agents are rationally inconsistent when they act immorally.[12]

---

10. As we will see, disagreement about what is the most proximate secondary metacause is the main difference between two theories about the ground of the moral order.

11. The distinction between natural and non-natural states of affairs is not always easily determined, however, as some are not obviously either one. Consider, for instance, the state of affairs *x is an act that is consistent with the design plan for human beings*. Is that a natural or non-natural state of affairs?

12. Alan Gewirth insists that moral agents who act immorally violate the "principle of categorial consistency." See Gewirth, *Reason and Morality*. The logical inconsistency of an immoral act arises because any agent, as an agent, in doing an act claims the right to act freely and purposively—and any one impacted by the act, as a potential agent, has

Principia Meta-Ethica

In *Principia Ethica* G. E. Moore identified what he called "the naturalistic fallacy," which he believed afflicted naturalist moral theories. The mistake, according to Moore, is to identify any non-moral property as identical to a moral property.[13] Moral properties, on Moore's account, are not identical with any non-moral property; they are simple and unanalyzable, like the property *being yellow*. As I have tried to show in chapter 2, however, moral theorists need not find a non-moral property and identify it with a moral property; all they need to do is to link these properties so that if something has the non-moral property it metacauses that it has the moral property. This metacausal relationship could hold even if moral properties are simple, non-reducible, and unanalyzable. So Moore's complaint was against a metaethical stance that moral theorists need not take, and a charitable reading does not understand them to be making such claims. But the "naturalistic fallacy" is poorly named for another reason. It is not a fallacy unique to naturalist moral theories at all—the purported error identified by Moore applies equally to naturalist and non-naturalist moral theories. Moore would have thought it a fallacy to say that the predicates "is commanded by God" and "is morally obligatory" each refer to the same property. Moore identified it as a fallacy just because he thought it a mistake to *identify* any moral property with a non-moral property of any kind. As I argued in chapter 2, he may be right about this, but typically moralists are not claiming that a non-moral property is identical to some moral property.

In the next two sections of this chapter, I consider briefly one naturalist theory about the grounding of the moral order—natural law, and one non-naturalist theory—the divine command theory.

Natural Law

Natural law is an idea that has a long history in metaethics, and it is has been the most important version of moral realism. The view associated with it was first articulated clearly by the Stoics, and in particular by the Roman statesman Cicero. It became the view of Western Christianity through

---

the same rights. An immoral act is one that denies any potential agents the rights that the agent of the act implicitly claims for himself in doing the act.

13. "The naturalistic fallacy is the assumption that because the words 'good' and, say, 'pleasant' necessarily describe the same objects, they must attribute the same quality to them." Prior, *Logic*, 1.

the influence of Augustine and especially, Thomas Aquinas. Although it was challenged in the modern period by philosophers like Thomas Hobbes, up until the last hundred years or so it had been the dominant metaethical view in the West. It is a view that combines an ontological and an epistemological component. Ontologically, it is the view that human beings all have the same nature and that moral obligations are grounded in this nature. As such, human beings are equal, and moral obligations are the same for all persons. Because moral obligations are based on human nature, they are logically prior to any social norms or legal requirements. Epistemologically, natural law normally includes the idea that humans can determine the basic obligations of the moral order from knowledge of human nature. (Of course, any view of the grounding of the moral order should imply that persons can know the basic obligations, at least in principle, since precepts that *cannot* be known are not binding. The claim that ignorance of the law is no excuse is accurate only when the law could have been known.) My interest here, however, is not about the epistemological commitments that normally are part of natural law. The issue of the grounding of the moral order is an ontological issue, so for now we can ignore the epistemological features of natural law. But using the term "natural law" when speaking of that view without its normal epistemological commitments may be misleading, since that is such an important part of how the term is typically understood. For the sake of clarity, I will use the term *natural ordinances* to refer only to the ontological component of natural law.

The natural ordinances view is that human beings have a nature, that is, they have a particular design and purpose. Of course, animals also have a particular design and purpose. In high school biology when a student dissects a frog, the operative assumption is that all frogs of the same species share a common design, so by examining just one frog one learns about the physiology of all such frogs. In behavioral science, watching one group of frogs suffices to make general statements about how frogs of the same species behave. Frogs of the same species share a design and purpose. If one came upon a frog that tried to walk on his back legs and attempted to eat flowers rather than insects, one would immediately say the frog was not acting like a frog of that species should.

Simply put, a natural ordinances view of the immediate ground of the moral order is that there are ways for human being to act that are fitting for beings with the design and purpose that human beings have. What is unique about human acts, as opposed to the behavior of frogs or any other animal, is that humans can act in ways that are contrary to their nature. Animals cannot help but behave in accord with their nature, but human beings have the freedom to choose to act in ways that are contrary to their nature. The natural ordinances view grounds the moral order so that acts which are consistent with human design and purpose are morally permissible, and acts that are contrary to that design or inhibit that purpose are morally impermissible. Natural ordinances views have, in general, an explanatory moral principle which includes some claim that an act that is consistent with human design and purpose metacauses that the act is morally permissible.[14] The way in which the moral principles of natural ordinance theories differ depends on the specific way in which each one identifies the design and purpose of human persons. For example, a moral theorist could hold that the purpose of each human is to achieve happiness. For another it is to be rational, and for yet another it is to glorify God—and there are many other possibilities. Each of these theories holds that the design and purpose of human beings—however it is identified—is the immediate ground of the moral order.[15]

Objections to Natural Law/Natural Ordinances

For classical moralists natural law has been one of the main views regarding the grounding of the moral order. The view that the moral order is grounded in the design and purpose of human beings has a long and distinguished history in the West, although it has fallen into disrepute by many contemporary moralists. One objection levied against it focuses on the idea that human beings have a specific and common human nature—a common design and purpose. In the late modern era doubts about the existence of a common human nature were introduced by existentialism. Existentialism said that human beings have radical freedom, so that each individual has the opportunity to define for himself or herself what kind of being he or she chooses to be. The only un-human choice was not to choose at all, but to abandon oneself to the strictures imposed by others. In postmodern philosophical anthropology, the idea that all human beings have a common

---

14. Or that expresses the materially equivalent principle that an act inconsistent with human design and purpose metacauses that the act is morally impermissible.

15. Here it is worth pointing out that one need not be a theist to believe that persons have a common human nature and that some acts are appropriate for beings with this nature and some acts are not.

design and purpose is no longer an accepted idea; the focus has turned to issues of social environments and their influence on persons and relationships between persons.

Another common objection made to natural law ethics is based on the epistemological issues with the theory. How does one know what the specific natural laws are that metacause specific moral precepts? Natural laws seem as evasive as moral precepts, so it does not help to explain the latter by using the former. Roman Catholic ethics has been more confident in the ability of human beings to deduce precepts of the moral order from the design and purpose of human persons, especially by considering what each human person wants and needs. Human beings desire and need water, so water is a good for human beings. Since water is a moral good, every person has a moral right to it, and thus everyone has a moral obligation not to violate a person's right to water. Not all Christians find this reasoning foolproof; Protestants argue that sin has so affected humanity that human desires are corrupted and an unreliable guide to what is good.[16] Whether this objection has merit, or how much merit it has, is not at issue here. The thing to note is that it is an objection to an epistemological feature of natural law and, thus, is not at issue in the natural ordinances view presently being considered since that view makes no epistemological commitments. Protestants and Roman Catholics may agree that the moral order is grounded in human nature as created by God without any commitment as to how we come to know it.

A third objection to the natural ordinances view is based on a theological position. Most theists hold that God is almighty and has perfect freedom to rule as he chooses. Yet the natural ordinances theory limits the moral laws that God can issue to those which are appropriate or fitting for human nature. God does not have the sovereignty to command whatever he wills. Thus one theistic objection to the natural ordinances view is that it diminishes God's power and freedom. It limits God to commanding those acts that are suited to human nature, and the objection is that no theory that limits God is possibly true. This desire to preserve and maintain God's absolute power and freedom is commendable, but I think we can preserve God's sovereignty while holding to the natural ordinances view.

---

16. This objection has some merit in the abstract, since persons often have bad desires, although it seems to me that we can know some desires are good and do generate moral obligations.

If we think of the moral order as a kind of owner's manual for a new Ford, where operating the Ford according to the manual is the analog of living a moral life, consider these questions: when Ford manufactures a vehicle, say a Mustang, can it put whatever it wants into the owner's manual? Is it sovereign with respect to the contents of the owner's manual? Of course, before the Mustang is designed and built Ford could engineer it in such a way as to conform to some predetermined owner's manual, however after the Mustang is produced there is an appropriate way to operate it. Ford's options for what it can put in the owner's manual end when the car is manufactured. At that point in time Ford has to say what is best for the car as produced. There is a standard for what the owner's manual should say that is external to Ford. The instructions in the owner's manual are grounded in the design of the car as produced. Once the car is manufactured, Ford does not have the freedom to print whatever it wants in the owner's manual. In an analogous way, the natural ordinances view holds that having freely created human beings with the design and purpose we have, God is no longer absolutely free to command whatever he wills; rather, his commands are a consequence of the nature with which he has created persons, and because God is good those commands reveal the best way to conduct a human life. The limits on God's power and freedom, if they should even be called that, are simply to always command the best for human persons with the nature he freely chose to create.

John E. Hare argues that "there is no necessary connection between our created natures and the way we reach our final ends."[17] He illustrates this with examples of possible but bizarre worlds in which things are very different than they actually are. In one, humans do not reproduce sexually but appear spontaneously as young adults; in another humans do not talk but only engage in wordless contemplation.[18] In such worlds, Hare argues, some of the moral obligations we would have would be different from the ones we now have. From this he concludes that from human nature alone one cannot deduce the moral obligations we have.

Hare's examples are imaginative, and his conclusion is true for moral rules, but it is mistaken when applied to moral precepts. Such precepts are true and binding in every possible world that is proximate to the actual world. They are grounded in what a human person is. The moral rules that are consistent with moral precepts will often vary. The moral rules would

17. Hare, *God's Call*, 68.
18. Ibid., 67.

Grounding the Moral Order

vary quite a lot if human persons were designed very differently from how in fact we are designed. If humans subsisted on birch tree bark, we might have a moral obligation to plant birch trees, or protect birch trees. If human persons had been given very strange new possible features, those new attributes very well could metacause some very different ways we would carry out moral obligations. It is even possible that the possible changes are so radical that some moral precepts themselves could be different from what they are. But this only shows that many true moral precepts only have *proximate world necessity*, as explained in chapter 4. To do what is required by moral principles (and moral precepts) usually involves a consideration of contingent factors. For instance, the moral precept *Never put any person at unnecessary physical risk of harm* means that in Kenya a person driving a vehicle should obey the local law and drive on the left side of the road. The same moral precept applied in the U.S.A. requires a vehicle operator to drive on the right side of the road. This does not mean that the moral order is unrelated to human nature; it only means that how a person carries out his or her moral obligations often depends on contingent factors. It is not a moral precept to drive on the left side of the road in Kenya; it is a moral rule. Moral precepts are binding and true regardless of where a person is or who a person is, as long as the possible world is proximate to this world. The application of a moral precept in a particular society depends on contingent factors in the society, including what is legally permitted and what is not. Hare's error seems to be conflating moral rules with moral precepts. It is true that we cannot know moral rules by only considering human nature, as his examples show, but he does not show that we cannot know any moral precepts from knowing the design and purpose of human persons.[19]

A Christian who holds the natural ordinances view does not deny that God commands the moral order, but on this view the commanding is not the immediate ground of the moral order. In fact, the moral order is what grounds God's command, that is, God commands it because it is true, and it is true because of human design and purpose. So God's commanding the moral order is his informing us as to the content of the order, not the way in which the moral order itself is grounded. The conclusion to be drawn is that if human beings do share a common nature, a common design and

---

19. Even if Hare were able to show that we cannot know moral precepts from a consideration of human nature alone, it would not undercut the natural ordinances view which specifically avoids any epistemological commitments.

purpose, then the view that the moral order is metacaused by that shared nature is both reasonable and defensible.

Divine Command Theory

While a person could hold to the natural ordinances view regarding the grounding of the moral order without being a theist, this is not the case for divine command theories. As their name implies, divine command theories require belief in the existence of God or gods. It would have been the view expressed by Euthyphro had he answered Socrates by saying that morally right acts are morally right because the gods love them (and so command them), but this was so contrary to Greek thought that Plato could not envision Euthyphro choosing this option, although Socrates offers it to him. Divine command theories are so-named because they identify the immediate ground of the moral order as God's command(s) regarding human conduct. As noted above, many who hold to a divine command theory object to the natural ordinances view because it seems to limit what God can command. If God is sovereign, they argue, he can command whatever he pleases. Thus, divine command theorists insist that God can do whatever he wills and is not limited by human nature—even if he is the one who created it. God commands whatever he chooses, and he is free to mandate any moral order. God is God, and what he chooses to command is not subject to any limitations due to considerations of human nature or consequences.

In its most radical form, of course, this means that it is within God's sovereign authority to command that persons murder and hate one another. He has not done this, of course, but he could have, and he still may. The moral order is only as fixed as God's commands, and he is free to change them. Some divine command moralists say that God's goodness sets limits on what commands he can give. One difficulty with this response is understanding what it means for God to be good if his commands are what determine the boundaries of conduct. Clearly God is good if his will determines what the good is and if he only does what he wills. But this is to be good by definition, and therefore not very informative. In a similar way the moral precept *murder is morally impermissible* is true because murder is defined as an unlawful killing; it is true by definition. The issue then becomes determining whether a particular event act-token is an instance of murder. It may be that God is good in ways that are completely different from how we are good, so if he commands that we should murder each other it does not impugn his goodness—but then what does it mean to say that God is good? On most divine command theories, God's commands are limited (if that's the right word) by some of his other attributes, like his goodness or his nature. The important point is that his commands are not limited by anything external to himself. Since he is loving and good, he cannot command hatred and murder.

One consequence of this view is that human beings cannot learn the contents of the moral order by considering natural reasons why some act may be permitted or not. God's commands are not limited by anything external to himself, and so the kinds of reasons that we have available to us play no role in what he commands. If a person wonders whether it is morally obligatory to pay taxes, it is irrelevant for her to consider whether the tax was fairly imposed, or whether the government does some socially positive things with the tax receipts, or whether it is something a good citizen would do. None of these reasons are relevant because God's commands are only limited by attributes of his nature, and none of these reasons are about his nature. The moral order is God's doing, and he produced it of his own free will. If any other factors weigh in on why God commands as he does, then his choice of what to command would be limited by those factors.

Thus there is an epistemological difference between the natural ordinance theory and the divine command theory. As a purely ontological view, the former is compatible with alternative epistemological views. One could hold that the moral order is or is not able to be discerned from considerations of human nature. The divine command theory, however, disallows the possibility that a human being can discern the moral order from considerations of human nature or any other considerations because God's commands themselves are not grounded in anything outside of himself. So while the question of the grounding of the moral order is not an epistemological issue, the answer given to the question may entail some epistemological commitments. The divine command theorist who is committed to God's sovereignty is committed to the epistemological view that nothing outside of God's nature sets any limits on what he commands, and so the moral order is not linked to the kind of creatures human beings are or the kind of world in which we live.

The important difference between the two theories, however, is not epistemological. A natural ordinance view, like a divine command theory, could hold that we know the moral order only through God's revealing it and agree that deductions from human nature are not sufficient for moral knowledge. A theistic natural ordinance theory has God's creation of human beings as a more remote secondary (meta)cause of the moral order—as the designer of human nature and as the creator of human beings. He could have created free creatures with a nature different from the one we have, and then the moral order would have been different. Having created human beings with the nature they have, the moral order is grounded in that created nature. In addition, one could hold that God is the one who reveals the moral order by his commands. The divine command theory is easier to explain: it is a theistic view in which God's commands are the immediate ground of the moral order, which he then reveals to us.

Does the Moral Order Have a Single Kind of Ground?

Do we need to choose between a natural ordinance and a divine command view of the ground of the moral order? For that matter, do we need to choose between a naturalist and a non-naturalist view? The answer to both of these questions is "no," but the reasons why require some explanation.

As stated earlier, explanatory moral principles identify the ground of the moral order when they say what non-moral state of affairs is the metacause of a moral state of affairs. A state of affairs is what a proposition expresses, and propositions can be simple or compound. And a state of affairs can be simple or compound. Recall Mill's view that the metacause of the moral order is the state of affairs expressed by the proposition *no other act y the agent could do instead of x has a higher utility than x has*. Assuming utility is something that can be measured, this state of affairs is empirically discernible and thus Mill's view is a kind of naturalism. I'm not sure whether Mill's view of the metacause of the moral order is simple or compound, so let's supplement it and make it clearly compound. Let's imagine a view of the non-moral state of affairs that metacauses the moral order to be *there is no other act y an agent could do instead of x that has a higher utility than x has and the act is permitted by God*. On this view the state of affairs that metacauses the moral order is compound, part of which is natural and part of which is non-natural.

In *Principia Ethica* G. E. Moore says that moral properties are simple and non-reducible, like *being yellow*, from which it seems to follow that some moral states of affairs are *simple*, that is, they are not compounds of two states of affairs. Perhaps Moore is right about moral properties, and about some moral states of affairs. But this does not imply that the

Grounding the Moral Order

non-moral state of affairs that metacauses a moral state of affairs must be a simple state of affairs. In fact, many of the proposals for the non-moral state of affairs that metacauses the moral order, like Kant's or Mill's, have been complicated—requiring pages of explanation—which suggests that they are compound.

The moral order may be grounded by a compound state of affairs. Let's say that the moral order is grounded by the non-moral state of affairs expressed in the compound proposition *p or q*. Now consider two moral states of affairs V and W. By definition, V and W are each grounded by P or Q. Let's further suppose that V is immediately grounded by P, and W is immediately grounded by Q. In such a case, it is true that V and W are both grounded by the same state of affairs expressed by *p or q*; it is also true that V is grounded in the state of affairs P and W is ground by Q. Thus it is possible for a compound state of affairs to be the ground of the moral order; more important, it shows that different states of affairs in the compound non-moral state of affairs (expressed by disjuncts or conjuncts) may metacause different specific precepts of the moral order. If we have a compound state of affairs A, and part of A is state of affairs B, and B is the immediate metacause of a moral state of affairs R, the inclination is to call B the ground of R, because A is a more remote metacause.

What this shows is that it may be a mistake to think that the entire moral order is grounded in any one simple state of affairs. It is possible that different precepts in the moral order are grounded in different non-moral states of affairs, and the whole moral order is only grounded by a compound metacause including all these different states of affairs. This possibility is not surprising. We are accustomed to sets of rules being grounded on different bases. Parents make some rules in order to protect a child from harm, such as *You may not go out of the backyard*, and other rules for different reasons, like *You must always kiss me goodnight before going to bed*. To a child these are both requirements, and they have equal binding force. But clearly the ground for each of the rules is different. Governments also enact positive laws on a variety of grounds. Some are to protect the public interest, yet others are for the benefit of some specific industry or a select group of persons. In a similar way, there is no reason to think that every part of the moral order has the same ground. Medieval Jewish philosophers regularly argued about the reasons or basis for the various laws of the Torah; using our present terminology, they discussed what grounds the laws of the Torah. Maimonides, the most important of the Jewish medieval philosophers, divided the laws of the Torah into those grounded in welfare of the body and those grounded in the welfare of the soul.[20] But he found some laws that did not seem to be grounded in either of these. The fact that the Torah has multiple grounds illustrates that it is not unusual to consider sets of rules as having different kinds of grounds.

The possibility that the moral order is not grounded in one simple non-moral state of affairs can be seen if we can identify two moral precepts that are metacaused by different non-moral states of affairs. One moral precept is *stealing is morally impermissible*. We may not agree on what this precept is grounded on—it is possibly metacaused by God's command or in human nature, or perhaps there is another alternative. Another moral obligation is that every person has a moral obligation to worship God or *worshipping God is morally obligatory*. God could not command us *not* to worship him, nor could he create any free creatures who would not have that obligation. Thus the metacause for this moral obligation is not God's command, nor is it human nature, rather the precept is grounded in God's great and unsurpassable glory. The ground of the moral obligation to worship God is God's nature itself. So there are at least two different grounds for moral precepts and we can see the possibility that the grounding of the moral order is compound.[21]

The claim that the ground of the moral order may be compound can be seen in another way. Part of the moral order is any true explanatory moral principle. Now consider whether an explanatory moral principle is itself metacaused by the non-moral state of affairs that it identifies. Does it identify its own ground? Not obviously. If one holds to, say, an explanatory moral principle expressing some version of the natural ordinance view, it is possible and even reasonable to hold the view that the ground of the principle itself is God's free will to ground moral precepts on the design and purpose of human persons. If this moral theory is true, then part of the moral order is grounded in God's free will and part of it is grounded in the design and purpose of human beings. If this moral theory is even possible, then it is possible that the moral order has a compound ground.

20. Maimonides, *Guide*, 406–7.

21. Some may prefer to distinguish religious and moral obligations, but in the Christian West for the most part theologians (for instance, John Calvin) considered all the obligations of the first table of the Ten Commandments (actions directed to God) and the second table (actions directed to human persons) to be moral obligations. Insofar as the moral order regulates all voluntary and purposive acts (cf. chapter 5), it includes religious choices as well.

Conclusion

Since it is possible that the ground of the moral order is compound, it is unwise for moralists to assume that the non-moral state of affairs that metacauses it is simple. In trying to identify the non-moral state of affairs of the moral order a more cautious strategy would be to consider the ground of a specific precept or sets of precepts—rather than assume that the whole moral order is grounded by one kind of non-moral state of affairs. A true explanatory moral principle may involve a fairly complex and compound non-moral state of affairs. It may well be the case that some moral precepts are grounded in divine commands and other moral precepts in natural ordinances. Thus, a simple version of either one of these may be mistaken.

Bibliography

Adams, Robert Merrihew. "A Modified Divine Command Theory of Ethical Wrongness." In *Religion and Morality*, edited by Gene Outka and John P. Reeder, 318–47. Garden City, NY: Anchor, 1973.
Aristotle. *Nicomachean Ethics*. In *The Basic Works of Aristotle*, edited by Richard McKeon and translated by W. D. Ross, 927–1112. New York: Random House, 1971.
Ayer, Alfred J. *Language, Truth and Logic*. 2nd. ed. New York: Dover, 1942.
Barna Group. "Americans are Most Likely to Base Truth on Feelings." https://www.barna.org/barna-update/article/5-barna-update/67-americans-are-most-likely-to-base-truth-on-feelings.
Churchill, Winston. "The Truth." http://www.brainyquote.com/quotes/quotes/w/winstonchu129864.html.
Cicero, Marcus Tullius. *De Legibus*. In *The Political Works of Marcus Tullius Cicero: Comprising his Treatise on the Commonwealth; and His Treatise on the Laws*, 1–171. Translated by Francis Barham. London: Spettigue, 1841–1842.
Clifford, William K. "The Ethics of Belief." *Contemporary Review* 29 (December 1876–May 1877) 289–309.
Donagan, Alan. "Is There a Credible Form of Utilitarianism?" In *Contemporary Utilitarianism*, edited by Michael D. Bayles, 187–202. Garden City, NY: Anchor, 1968.
———. *The Theory of Morality*. Chicago: University of Chicago Press, 1977.
Feldman, Fred. *Introductory Ethics*. Englewood Cliffs, NJ: Prentice-Hall, 1978.
Frankena, William K. *Ethics*. 2nd ed. Prentice-Hall Foundations of Philosophy Series. Englewood Cliffs, NJ: Prentice-Hall, 1973.
Gewirth, Alan. "Common Morality and the Community of Rights." In *Prospects for a Common Morality*, edited by Gene Outka and John P. Reeder, 29–52. Princeton: Princeton University Press, 1993.
———. *Reason and Morality*. Chicago: University of Chicago Press, 1978.
Hare, John E. *God's Call: Moral Realism, God's Commands, and Human Autonomy*. Grand Rapids: Eerdmans, 2001.
Hauerwas, Stanley. *The Peaceable Kingdom*. South Bend, IN: University of Notre Dame Press, 1983.
Himmelfarb, Gertrude. *The Demoralization of Society*. New York: Knopf, 1995.
Hume, David. *A Treatise of Human Nature*. London: Oxford University Press, 1902.
Lewis, C. S. *Mere Christianity*. New York: Macmillan, 1943.
———. *The Abolition of Man*. New York: Macmillan, 1947.

Bibliography

Maimonides, Moses. "A Guide for the Perplexed." In *Philosophy in the Middle Ages*, edited Arthur Hyman and James J. Walsh, 363–409. Indianapolis, IN: Hackett, 1973.

MacIntyre, Alasdair. *A Short History of Ethics*. 2nd ed. South Bend, IN: University of Notre Dame Press, 1998.

Moore, G. E. *Principia Ethica*. London: Cambridge University Press, 1966.

Outka, Gene. "Augustinianism and Common Morality." In *Prospects for a Common Morality*, edited by Gene Outka and John P. Reeder, 114–48. Princeton: Princeton University Press, 1993.

Outka, Gene, and John P. Reeder. *Prospects for a Common Morality*. Princeton: Princeton University Press, 1993.

Plantinga, Alvin. *The Nature of Necessity*. London: Oxford University Press, 1974.

———. *Warrant and Proper Function*. New York: Oxford University Press, 1993.

———. *Warranted Christian Belief*. New York: Oxford University Press, 2000.

———. *Where the Conflict Really Lies*. New York: Oxford University Press, 2011.

Plato. *Euthyphro*. In *The Collected Dialogues of Plato*, edited by Edith Hamilton and Huntington Cairns and translated by Lane Cooper, 169–85. Princeton: Princeton University Press, 1962.

Prior, A. N. *Logic And The Basis of Ethics*. London: Oxford University Press, 1949.

Rorty, Richard. "The Priority of Democracy to Philosophy." In *Prospects for a Common Morality*, edited by Gene Outka and John P. Reeder, 254–78. Princeton: Princeton University Press, 1993.

———. "Truth and Freedom: A Reply to Thomas McCarthy." In *Prospects for a Common Morality*, edited by Gene Outka and John P. Reeder, 279–90. Princeton: Princeton University Press, 1993.

Scarfe, Francis. "Romanticism." In *Encyclopedia Britannica*, 14th ed., s.v. Chicago: Encyclopedia Britannica, 1970.

Stob, Henry. *Ethical Reflections*. Grand Rapids: Eerdmans, 1978.

Yancey, Phillip. "Nietzsche Was Right." *Books and Culture* 4.1 (1998) 14–17.

Index of Topics

Abolition of Man, The (Lewis), 5, 109
absolute complements, 45–46
absolutizing, 3
acts
  moral vs. amoral, 100
  moral properties of, 49, 82, 98
  purposive, 102–3
  voluntary, 102
act-tokens, 35
  act-types as kinds of, 54–56
  attributing moral property to, 49–50
  as composites of other 50–51
  done on purpose, 56
  identifying and expressing, 50–57
  individuation of, 50
  as moral field, 88
  moral interest of, 50
  moral judgments and, 53–54
  morally neither good nor bad, 86–87
  moral principles and, 87
  moral properties and, 50–51, 55, 91–92, 98–99
  purposive, 102–3
  references to, 51–52
  voluntary, 100–102
act-types, 31, 35, 37, 49
  as categories of act-tokens, 54–56
  outside the moral field, 89, 99
  morality of, 57
adultery, 32
aesthetic beliefs, 116
aesthetic judgments, 106–12
agents, 13–14
amoral, identifying, 81–82
Analects (Confucius), 110n7

animals
  design and purpose of, 131
  moral properties of, 92
anthropology, philosophical, 132–33
antirealists, 38
a priori beliefs, 116
"at will," 56

behaviorism, philosophical, 100
beings-in-community, humans as, 2
beliefs
  evidence obligation and, 113
  formation of, 117–22
  kinds of, 116
bi-conditional, 64
broadly logical necessity, 78–79

Caiaphas's rule, 77
Calvin College, ix–x
categorical imperative, 62–63
causality, 70
causation, 126–28
CF, *see* classical foundationalism
child sacrifice, 3
choice, forced, 101
Christian faith, moral antirealism and, 17–18
classical foundationalism, 113
classicism, 17
coextensive, defined, 24–25
cognitive faculties, functioning of, 115–16
cognitivism, 23
  correctness of, 40

Index of Topics

cognitivism *(continued)*
   noncognitivists' arguments against, 25–34
   types of, 24–25
cognitivists, 11, 33–34
commands, acceptance of, 34
common morality, 1
   disagreement over, 1–9
   no prospects for, 2–4
   parts of, 1
   some prospects for, 4–6
   two concepts of, 7–8
common referents, 73
complements, types of, 45
complete moral field, 83–84, 88, 99
complete moral theory, 87
conditional sentences, 79
conscience, 116–22
consistency, as characteristic of the moral order, 15
constraints, external vs. internal, 101
constructivism, 10, 11–13
contingent statements, 22
counterfactuals, 53, 79–80
customs, 5

definism, 24, 25–28
definists, 38, 40
deontological moral theories, 96–97
design plan, 120–21, 122
desires
   moral views and, 32
   motive and, 32
divine command theory, 60n4, 75, 136–38
divine law, 125
divorce, 12

emotivism, 23, 24
empirical science, 17
empiricism, 22
Enlightenment, 17
epistemic environment, congenial, 118–20, 122
epistemology, 106
   philosophical, 112, 114
ethics, 37, 60, 92
   as independent science, x
   philosophical interest in, 12
Ethics (Frankena), 23
ethics of suspicion, 12
Euthyphro (Plato), 72, 125–26
Euthyphro Test, 127
event act-tokens, 51–53
events, moral properties of, 93–94
evidence obligation, 112–13
evidentialism, moral, 112–13
evolution, conscience and, 121–22
evolutionary theory, 17, 18
existentialism, 132
explanatory moral principles, 76, 77, 127–28, 138
expressivism, x, 10, 11, 23, 35, 105
expressivist hermeneutics, 37

false antecedents, 79
field conversion principles, 88, 96–99
final solution, Hitler's, 3
first cause, 126
flat tax, 15
foolishness, not believing, 112
foundationalism, classical, 113
freedom, restriction of, 101
French revolution, 17

globalization, moral antirealism and, 18
God
   goodness of, 136–37
   limits on, 133–34, 136–37
   nature of, 140
golden rule, 6, 7
grounding, 128–29

human nature, law of, 6
human rights, 3, 20
humans
   acting contrary to their nature, 132
   design and purpose of, 131, 132
   freedom of, 138
   as rational beings, 2
hypothetical particular moral judgments, 54

immediate ground, 129
immoral rules, 58

Index of Topics

imperativists, 34
inductive beliefs, 116
infanticide, 15
Introductory Ethics (Feldman), 62
intuition, 28–29
intuitionism, 24–25, 28–34
ius gentium, 8
ius naturale, 8

judgments
  aesthetic, 106–12
  moral, 106, 111–12, 116–17
justice, 4, 5, 7

knowability, as characteristic of the moral order, 15
knowledge, conditions for, 114

language, philosophy of, 34
Language, Truth and Logic (Ayer), 25
laws, basis for, 12
local rules, 5
logical equivalence, 45n4, 70, 72, 75
lying, 32–33

materialism, physical, 17
maximal net pleasure, 87
maximal relative complementarity, 60
maximal relative complements, 47–48
memory, 115–16
memory beliefs, 116
Mere Christianity (Lewis), 5
metacausality, 75–77, 87, 91, 127–28, 130
metaethics, ix, x, 1, 130
  classical view of, 4–6, 7
  postmodern view of, 2–4, 6–7
modal logic, 77
moral absolutes, 13
moral acts, 99–103
moral agents, 13, 101
moral antirealism, 9–11, 105–6
  changes leading to, 16–19
  consequences of, 21
  problems with, 19–21
  types of, 10, 11
moral antirealists, 16, 38, 105, 124–25

moral beliefs, 115, 116, 117–19
moral cognitivism, 10, 11
moral constructivism, 10, 11, 105–6
moral discernment, moral precepts and, 57
moral epistemology, x
  development of, 106
  main question of, 105
moral evidentialism, 112–13
moral evils, 94
moral expressivism, 10, 11
moral expressivists, 84
moral fields, 48–49, 61, 81. *See also* complete moral field
  acts and, 64
  difference in, 84
  identification of, 69
  identifying, 69, 81, 82
  moral principles and, 67, 69
  moral properties and, 64, 85
moral grounding, 68
moral hermeneutics, 22–23, 24, 34, 35, 38, 105n1
moral intuitionism, 28. *See also* intuitionism
moralists, kinds of, 105
morality, 7
  arising within community, 3
  binding, 1, 5, 6–8
  common, *see* common morality
  many versions of, 8
  normative, 8–9. *See also* moral order
  positive, 8–9
  social, 12
  traditional, 88n12
  two concepts of, 6–9
  universal, 5
moral judgments, 49, 50, 106, 111–12, 116–17
  act-tokens and, 53–54
  as emotional expressions, 24
  expressing an attitude, 24
  motivation and, 31
  prescriptive character of, 35
  as recommendations, 24
  translated into moral statements, 74
  truth value of, 22–23

Index of Topics

moral knowledge, warrant for, 113–22
moral language, x, 9, 10, 34
  elimination of, 74
  theories about, 23
moral law, universal, 4
morally bad, 41, 85, 88–96
morally good, 41, 85, 87n11, 88–96
morally impermissible, 41, 43, 44–49, 53, 54–55, 59, 61, 65, 85–88, 124
morally obligatory, 41, 43–44, 59, 62, 85–86, 95
morally permissible, 41, 43–49, 53, 54–55, 57, 59, 61, 65, 67, 85–88, 91, 103, 124
morally permissible rules, 57–58
morally right, 41, 43, 85, 87n11, 126
morally wrong, 41, 43, 85
moral noncognitivists, 38
moral obligations, 3
  grounded in natural law, 131
  sources of, 78
moral ontology, x
moral order, 9
  characteristics of, 14–16
  conduct for, discovery of, 13
  constructivism and, 11–13
  describing, 13–16
  ground of, 129–38
  grounding of, 124–25, 128, 138–40
  identifying, 16
  metacause of, 138
  moral reality and, 12
  necessity for, 20
  as owner's manual, 134
  standard of, 20
  understanding of, 59, 125
moral philosophy, as practical science, 34
moral possibility, future, 36
moral precepts, 35, 49, 54–57, 65
  common, in different societies, 6
  expression of, 99
  falsehood of, 57
  helpful, 57
  interpretation of, 37
  justifiability of, 7
  linked with moral judgments, 37–38
  meaning of, 37
  prioritizing, 44
  requirements for following, 135
  subject of, 54
  truth of, 37–38, 54, 55–56
  value of, limited, 57
moral predicates, x, 26, 29, 35
  attribution of, 84
  kinds of, 85
  moral properties and 99–100
  non-moral predicates and, 73–74
  referring to a property, 39
moral principles, 40, 49, 60
  as compound proposition, 66–67
  counter-examples to, 78–80
  differences between, 69
  dividing the moral field, 69
  effects of, 61
  examples of, 62
  form of, 69–70
  identifying moral field of the theory, 65
  kinds of, 76–77, 127
  linking, 69–72
  logical structure of, 61–64, 68–69
  meeting logical conditions, 60
  metacausality and, 76
  modality of, 60, 77–80
  moral field and, 64–68, 82–83
  moral properties and, 71
  necessity of, 77, 78–79
  options for, 87
  requirements for following, 135
  truth of, 79
  working for possible and actual situations, 77
moral properties, x
  acts and, 64
  attribution of, 30, 36, 49, 52–53
  characteristics of, 29
  common examples of, 41–42
  complementarity of, 44–47
  derived from each other, 41n1, 59n2
  expression of, 42–43
  intuition and, 29
  kinds of, 85
  moral field and, 85
  possession of, 81
  property variables and, 63

Index of Topics

sets of, 85–87
moral propositions
   modality of, 77–80
   types of, 49
moral realism, 9, 16–19, 130
moral realists, 105, 124–25
moral reality, 12
moral rules, 15, 57–58, 134–35. *See also* morally permissible rules
moral science, 97
moral statements, 22–23
moral system principles, 71, 76, 127
moral systems, false propositions in, 83
moral theory, 29, 40, 71. *See also* true moral theory
   basis for, 38
   complete, 83
   development of, 81
   essence of, 60
   identifying its moral field, 48
   kinds of, 96–97
   moral field of, 81
   need for, 15
   proposition of, 74–75
moral thought, Nietzche's influence on, 2
moral truths, denial of, 20
moral value, recognizing, 111–12
most proximate secondary cause, 126–27, 129
motivation, 31
motive, 31, 32
movies, moral properties of, 93–94
mutuality, among moral properties, 88

natural events, moral properties of, 94
naturalism, 25–26, 129, 138
naturalistic fallacy, x, 130
natural law, 60n4, 130–35
natural ordinance view, 131–36, 137–38
Nazis, 20–21, 118
Neoclassicism, 17
No Motivation Argument, 25, 28, 30–34
non-basic beliefs, 113
noncognitivism, 23–24, 35–40
noncognitivists, 11

non-moral predicate, 26, 29
non-moral properties, 69
   identifying with moral properties, 72–75
   moral properties and, 69–72, 130
   property variables and, 63
non-naturalism, 25, 129
normative morality, 8–9. *See also* moral order
normative moral theories, 44

objectivity, as characteristic of the moral order, 14
objects, moral properties of, 93–94
obligations, moral, 3
open question, 26–27
Open Question Argument, 25–28, 29, 34, 39–40, 72–73, 74

particular moral judgments, 35–38. *See also* moral judgment
perceptual beliefs, 116
personal agent, 13
persons
   character statements about, 91
   moral fields and, 86
   moral properties of, 89–92, 98
philosophers, process of, 73
philosophical anthropology, 132–33
philosophical behaviorism, 100
philosophical epistemology, 106, 112, 114
pleasure, 25, 26, 87
political issues, 15–16
polygamy, 10
positive laws, 15
positive morality, 8–9
possible worlds, 77n25, 79–80
predicates, synonymy of, 39–40
prescriptivism, 23, 24
Principia Ethica (Moore), ix, 29, 95, 130, 138–39
pro-attitude, 31
properly basic beliefs, 113
properties, coextensive, 39
property variables, 63
propositions, expressing states of affairs, 95

Index of Topics

Prospects for a Common Morality (ed. Outka and Reeder), 1
Protestants, on human desire, 133
proximate possible worlds, 79
proximate-world necessity, 80, 135
purposiveness, 102–3

racism, 19
rationalist moral theory, 129
reason, motive as, 32
relative complements, 45, 46–48, 60–61
Republic (Plato), 109–10
rights, human, 3, 20
Roman Catholic ethics, 133
romanticism, 17
Rta, 110n7
rules, 57–58, 139
rule utilitarianism, 77–78

scientific learning, 17
secondary causes, 126, 128
Sensible Question Argument, 25, 28, 29–30, 34, 40
Short History of Ethics, A (MacIntyre), 3
silver rule, 5
sin, 133
Sittlichkeit, 2
social constructivists, 11–13
social conventions, intentionality of, 12
social morality, 12, 105–6, 125
  diversity of, 18
  existence of, 16
social norms, 15
social opinion, 118
states of affairs
  compound, 139
  as moral field, 87
  moral properties of, 95–99
  natural and non-natural, 129n11
Stoics, 130
subjectivism, 26
suicide, 56
superpersonal agent, 13–14

supervenience, 70–71
synonymy, 73

Tao, the, 6, 110–11
tax laws, 15–16
teleological moral theories, 95–97
theism, natural ordinances view and, 133, 135–36
Theory of Morality, The (Donagan), 56
Torah, 139–40
transcendence, as characteristic of the moral order, 15–16
trans-cultural truth, 3n6, 6
true moral field, 87
true moral theory, 83–84, 88
truth, trans-cultural, 3n6, 6

universality, as characteristic of the moral order, 14–15
utilitarianism, 26, 39
utility, moral principles and, 62

value
  judgment of, 107–12
  standard of, 110–11
values, 2
verificationism, 22
virtue ethics, 89
virtue theories, 87, 98
voluntariness, 100–102

warrant, 114–16, 122–23
Warrant: The Current Debate (Plantinga), 114
Warranted Christian Belief (Plantinga), x, 114
Warrant and Proper Function (Plantinga), 114
words
  expressing a property, 42–43
  meaning of, 38, 39–40, 42–43
Wordsworth, William, 110n7
wrongness, ethical, 75

Index of Authors

Adams, Robert Merrihew, 75
Aquinas, Thomas, 4, 16, 131
Aristotle, 4, 11, 34, 89, 97, 109, 110
Augustine, 4, 5–6, 7, 109, 131
Ayer, A. J., 24, 25–26, 39, 84n7

Booth, John Wilkes, 49, 50, 51

Calvin, John, 140n21
Carson, Johnny, 106–7
Churchill, Winston, 19
Cicero, 4–5, 6, 7, 8, 130
Clifford, W. K., 112

Dennett, Daniel, 120n25
Donagan, Alan, ix, 4, 56, 77–78, 88n12

Euthyphro, 125–26, 127

Feldman, Fred, 62, 65, 82
Flew, Anthony, 112
Frankena, William K., 23–25, 26, 28, 30, 31, 39

Gewirth, Alan, 4, 7, 8, 16, 100–101, 102–3, 129
Gratian, 8

Hare, John E., 26, 35, 70, 134, 135
Hare, R. M., 70
Hauerwas, Stanley, 8
Hegel, G. W. F., 2
Himmelfarb, Gertrude, 2
Hitler, Adolf, 3
Hobbes, Thomas, 131

Hume, David, 30, 112

Isidore of Seville, 8

Kant, Immanuel, 2, 4, 16, 63, 65, 77, 87, 139
Konyndyk, Ken, ix

Lewis, C. S., 4, 5–6, 8, 109–12
Lincoln, Abraham, 49, 50, 51
Locke, John, 112

MacIntyre, Alasdair, 3–4
Maimonides, 139–40
Mill, J. S., 4, 16, 62–63, 65, 73, 74–75, 77, 82, 87, 138, 139
Moore, G. E., ix, x, 26, 29, 87, 95, 98, 130, 138–39
Mouw, Richard, ix

Nietzsche, Friedrich, 2, 12

Outka, Gene, 1, 21

Plantinga, Alvin, ix, x, 78n28, 101–2, 112–13, 114–16, 120–21, 122
Plato, 4, 11, 72n21, 109–10, 125–26, 136
Price, Vincent, 106–7, 109

Reeder, John P., 1, 21
Rorty, Richard, 2–4
Rousseau, Jean-Jacques, 17
Russell, Bertrand, 112

Index of Authors

Scriven, Michael, 112
Socrates, 72n21, 125–26
Stevenson, C. L., 24
Stob, Henry, 88n12

Traherne, Thomas, 109

Ulpian, 8

Weber, Max, 2
Wolterstorff, Nicholas, ix

Yancey, Phillip, 19

www.ingramcontent.com/pod-product-compliance
Lightning Source LLC
Chambersburg PA
CBHW051940160426
43198CB00013B/2237